THE MATCHING PAIR
Part 1
NO GOOD DEED

by
Allan Warren

BUNNYWAR BOOKS

First published in 2021
by Bunnywar Books, London

'It's not easy in the theatre'
-Kit

The Matching Pair - Part 1: No Good Deed

Characters in order of appearance.

HARVEY CECIL-MILLER

Aristocratic, charming, handsome and fit. In his late twenties.

BASIL HOPKINS

Handsome, slightly overweight. Lower middle class. In his late twenties.

WOLFGANG (RECEPTIONIST)

Late fifties, portly. With a thick white moustache.

HANS ECKMANN

Dark haired, very fit, average good looks, in his early twenties.

GÜNTER SCHULER

Blond, fit, very good looking, in his early twenties.

COUNT VON GANTZ

Aritistocratic, elegant, in his early forties.

SS. MAN

Fit, in his mid thirties

EVA GOODMANN

Dark haired, slim, pretty, in her early twenties.

ACT I, SCENE I

EARLY AFTERNOON. THE LOBBY OF A SMALL HOTEL IN A SUBURB OF BERLIN. THE DECORATION IS BAVARIAN IN STYLE, WITH HUNTING TROPHIES ADORNING THE WOODEN PANELLING. STAGE RIGHT, IS THE ENTRANCE. UP-STAGE CENTRE, IS A LARGE WOODEN FIREPLACE WITH A BOAR'S HEAD ABOVE IT. EITHER SIDE OF THE FIREPLACE ARE TWO TYROLEAN STYLE WOODEN CHAIRS. DOWN-STAGE CENTRE ARE TWO RED LEATHER ARMCHAIRS, A COUPLE OF SIDE TABLES AND A COFFEE TABLE. UP-STAGE LEFT IS A WOODEN STAIRCASE LEADING UP TO A LANDING. STAGE LEFT IS THE RECEPTION DESK. BEHIND THE RECEPTION DESK IS A PAINTING OF ADOLPH HITLER DRAPED WITH A SWASTIKA FLAG. DOWN-STAGE RIGHT THERE IS A LARGE WINDOW.

HARVEY: *(HARVEY enters followed by BASIL who is weighed down with luggage)* Oh, don't be such a nincompoop, Basil!

BASIL: It's alright for you, Harvey, you're only carrying the passports. *(BASIL follows HARVEY to the reception desk. No one is at reception, so HARVEY taps a bell on the desk. BASIL seems exhausted and appears to be sweating. BASIL puts down their suitcases, and sits on one of them)* I do appreciate you inviting me along on these jaunts, Harvey. But why is it, whenever we go on a trip, I end up as your dogsbody?

HARVEY: Oh, do stop whinging, Basil. After all, it is give and take, you know. You do get a free holiday for just carrying the bags. *(HARVEY looks around impatiently)* Where is everybody? *(HARVEY glances back at BASIL sitting on the case)* Must you sit on the luggage? *(HARVEY then notices BASIL is sitting on his suitcase)* Damn it all, man, you're sitting on my Louis Vuitton! *(HARVEY turns back to the reception desk and taps the bell again. He then looks around the lobby)* Basil, be honest... do I look twenty years younger?

BASIL: Not by any stretch of the imagination. Anyway, that would make you nine years old. But then to be fair, in may ways, mentally you still are.

HARVEY: I've heard you can be very funny at times, but what I've yet to fathom, is why I've never been around at those particular times. *(HARVEY points at the decoration)* What I mean't was, this place is a veritable time capsule. I feel I've gone back in time, at least twenty years.

BASIL: *(BASIL looks around)* More like fifty, I would say, even before the Kaiser's time.

HARVEY: *(finally the RECEPTIONIST appears. He is dressed in a traditional Bavarian style jacket)* Ah, at last! Mein Lieber. *(RECEPTIONIST is not amused by the remark)* You have my booking? The Honourable Harvey Cecil-Miller, and one for my assistant, Basil Hopkins. *(the RECEPTIONIST looks over at BASIL, who is resting on the luggage, waving his trilby hat in the air, in order to cool himself. As the RECEPTIONIST begins searching for their booking. HARVEY notices BASIL is still sitting on his Louis Vuitton suitcase)* Basil, I said get off my case! If you have to slump, at least do it on your own suitcase. Better still, go sit in one of those chairs. *(HARVEY gestures toward the red leather chairs)* It'll stop that large gluteus maximus of yours from crushing my baggage.

RECEPTIONIST: *(RECEPTIONIST coldly)* I don't see any booking under either of your names.

HARVEY: But there has to be. The Honourable Harvey Cecil-Miller. I am a journalist. I'm here to cover the opening of the games tomorrow. Look again. The booking was made by my magazine, *The Pictorial*. You must have heard of it? You might even have heard of me? I'm pretty well known… well, in London anyway...

BASIL: *(BASIL mutters as he gets up and heads toward the chairs)* ... especially by most of the barmen, guardsmen and rent-boys.

RECEPTIONIST: I see, ja. Nein, ich habe nichts! *(the RECEPTIONIST looks at the register again)* Ja, now. *(In a patronising voice)* Sie sind Journalisten für das Frauenmagazin?

HARVEY: Yes, spot on, old boy. I am a journalist and you are correct again. It is a woman's magazine that I work for… but I don't know why you're being so sniffy about it? As it goes, it's a very popular magazine. Not just for women. Men also have been known to dip into it. Married men especially. *(HARVEY smiles and winks at him)* I think they like the lingerie section.

RECEPTIONIST: *(The RECEPTIONIST carries on what he is doing and mumbles to himself)* Geschwätz, Geschwätz.

HARVEY: Chatter, chatter? Oh, you mean gossip? Well, it's not all gossip and knitting patterns. There is a cookery section. It's also packed with exclusive interviews and photographs of all kinds of famous film stars, Charlie Chaplin, Cary Grant, Mae West, you name them.

RECEPTIONIST: *(doesn't bother to look up, he just nods in agreement in order to stop HARVEY talking)* Ja, ja, ja.

HARVEY: We've even had a German on the cover. *(the RECEPTIONIST looks up)* Marlene Dietrich? It sold out within two days. *(the RECEPTIONIST is unimpressed, so continues what he was doing)* Well maybe you'd like crosswords? It has an excellent crossword.

RECEPTIONIST: Nein. *(still shows no interest and continues searching his paperwork)*

HARVEY: Admittedly, it's not up to the standard of *The Times* crossword of course.

RECEPTIONIST: *(obviously irritated by the constant interruption)* Ja, ja,ja.

HARVEY: I'm told, it's the husbands who finish them... no doubt, to take their minds off their wives ruining my recipe suggestions.
RECEPTIONIST: *(the RECEPTIONIST interrupts, as he has at*

last found the booking) Passports! *(BASIL jumps up and heads back to the reception area. HARVEY hands over their passports. The RECEPTIONIST examines their passports)* Sign here! *(HARVEY and BASIL sign the register. As they do, the RECEPTIONIST scrutinizes their passports again)*

HARVEY: Also, I think you have an envelope for me? It's from your Ministry of Sport.

RECEPTIONIST: Nein!

HARVEY: No? Well, It's very important, so can you please check again? It'll be our tickets for the opening of the games tomorrow.

RECEPTIONIST: Nein, kein Briefumschlag. Keine Tickets!

HARVEY: But they said they would be waiting here when we checked in. *(to BASIL)* Crumbs, he doesn't have them!

RECEPTIONIST: Setzen Sie sich, während ich suche!

HARVEY: *(to BASIL)* He wants us to sit over there, while he sorts it out. *(HARVEY gestures toward the red leather chairs)* Good idea. We might as well be comfortable while we wait. *(HARVEY looks back at the RECEPTIONIST)* Perhaps you could bring us over a bottle of your delicious Spätlese trocken?

RECEPTIONIST: *(RECEPTIONIST is still miserable)* Ja, immediately.

HARVEY: *(as HARVEY and BASIL head over to the chairs, HARVEY checks for any damage to his suitcase)* You'll like the Spätlese. The aroma has just a hint of pear... or is it honeysuckle? Either way, it's not sweet, like some German wines. I suppose, it's rather like my suitcase, an elegant little number... that is, until you sat on it.

BASIL: Stop being such a prissy poof Harvey. I could hardly have crushed it, there's not an ounce of fat on me, let alone on my bum.

HARVEY: *(laughs as they slump down into the chairs)* I can certainly vouch for that old dear. First hand knowledge remember?

BASIL: What are you on about now?

HARVEY: Happy memories of Cambridge, old ducks..

BASIL: There were many.

HARVEY: What about the night you shimmied up my drain pipe?

BASIL: Oh, that? Well that certainly wasn't one of them. Here we go, you must be desperate, if you're going to drag up that old chestnut. From what little I remember, that was just one very blurred unhappy memory.

HARVEY: On the contrary, the very thought of you shimmying up my drainpipe, was a very happy one for me.

BASIL: *(laughs)* That's an unfortunate way of putting it. Be fair I didn't know it was your drainpipe. Otherwise, I certainly wouldn't have gone anywhere near it. Anyway, that's nearly ten years ago now.

HARVEY: Ah, so you don't deny it?

BASIL: No, I don't. I only wish I could.

HARVEY: Or prizing open my window, whipping off your clothes and leaping butt naked onto my bed?

BASIL: I really can't remember. As I said, it's just all one big horrible blur.

HARVEY: Conveniently so, no doubt.

BASIL: What is this? A trip down memory lane, to those so called halcyon days at Cambridge? That evening was a terrible mistake and yet you never let me live it down.

HARVEY: Terrible? At the time you loved it.

BASIL: It's obvious, your memory is solely dependent on your overly vivid and somewhat colourful imagination. I was well and truly pissed, remember? I didn't know where I was. You'd have been, too. After umpteen pints of brown ale, at the pub with Alice.

HARVEY: Ah yes, Alice, the sweet college nurse. *(HARVEY smirks)* How can I ever forget Alice. You following her home and yet, somehow miraculously ending up in bed with me.

BASIL: You're making me sound like a real pervert. Alice told me to follow her after she left the pub. She said her bedroom window would be open, so to climb up her drainpipe and get into her bed. Your building being right next to hers, and both your bedrooms on the first floor. It was an easy mistake to make.

HARVEY: Easy mistake? To think I was Alice? Alice, as round as a barrel, having had more rides than half the bikes in Cambridge?

BASIL: Of course, it was an easy mistake for anyone to make in my inebriated condition.

HARVEY: Perhaps, but I must say, it was a bit off-putting you calling me Alice all night.

BASIL: I was drunk.

HARVEY: Yes, you certainly were. You kept banging on about how you loved the smell of starch on my nurse's uniform. When in fact, all I was wearing was Aqua Velva aftershave and my silk polka dot boxers.

BASIL: What a thought.

HARVEY: Even so, you were rather passionate.

BASIL: For God's sake, spare me the details. You drag up that one drunken night, time and time and again.

HARVEY: To be honest, when I say passionate. Passionate might be just a tad of an exaggeration.

BASIL: Not that you'd be one to exaggerate, of course.

HARVEY: *(HARVEY smiles)* Well, when I say a tad. *(BASIL raises his eyes)* Oh, look at your face, dear old Basil, it's too cruel watching you squirm.

BASIL: Don't concern yourself, I'm used to it. Making me squirm seems to be your only real enjoyment in life.

HARVEY: Oh dear, how very sad for me, if that's true. Well maybe this is the perfect time to let you into a little secret. *(HARVEY chuckles)*

BASIL: What are you chuckling about now? Whatever it is, it's bound not to be funny!

HARVEY: Oh, but it is.

BASIL: To you maybe.

HARVEY: I promise, you'll find it hilarious when I tell you. But should I tell you, is the question?

BASIL: For pity's sake, spit it out, man!

HARVEY: *(continues laughing)* Okay. Well the truth is... are you ready for this?

BASIL: *(BASIL seemingly bored)* Yes, Harvey I'm ready for anything. Now just share your little joke, so we can both collapse hysterical with laughter... then, hopefully move on.

HARVEY: Well, the truth is... drum roll!

BASIL: Yes? And the truth is?

HARVEY: I've been winding you up for years! *(roars with laughter)* And what's more, everytime you fall for it.

BASIL: So what's new? What's so funny about that?
HARVEY: Because nothing happened. That's what's funny. In truth, you my dear Basil, you are still a fully fledged, hetrosexual

male. The nearest to passion you got that night, was passing out on my bed.

BASIL: Hold on. Seriously, nothing happened?

HARVEY: Seriously? I can even go as far as, honestly... no, nothing happened. Nada, Zilch! *(HARVEY grins)*

BASIL: Then you are one sick bastard! After all this time. You could have put me out of my misery years ago.

HARVEY: Yes, but where would have been the fun in that? You should be pleased. I thought you'd find it funny.

BASIL: On the contrary. I should be angry, but I'm too overcome with relief.

HARVEY: *(the RECEPTIONIST brings a tray with wine in an ice bucket and two glasses. He places them on the coffee table in front of the chairs)* Oh, good, the drinks!

RECEPTIONIST: Ich serviere?

HARVEY: Nein danke, mein Herr. We can pour it ourselves.

RECEPTIONIST: Gut, enjoy it! It is an excellent choice.

HARVEY: Am sure we will. Oh, good you brought plenty of ice. Danke, very efficient. By the way, any news on our tickets?

RECEPTIONIST: Nein.
HARVEY: Hmm, not so efficient. Please let us know immediately they arrive.

RECEPTIONIST: Ja, ja. *(the RECEPTIONIST goes back to the reception desk)*

BASIL: *(HARVEY pours the wine)* Were you really only wearing polka dot silk boxers?

HARVEY: *(HARVEY hands BASIL a glass)* Yes, why?

BASIL: *(BASIL takes a sip and pulls a face)* Yuck! That's the reason I gave up drinking brown ale, I kept getting these blurred flashbacks of you, prancing around in polka dot boxers. I thought it was down to the beer.

HARVEY: What do you mean? I've never pranced anywhere. Well, look at the good side. If the very sight of me in silk boxers, put you off drinking that ghastly stuff. Then your palate owes my boxers a debt of gratitude.

BASIL: It's true. Thanks to you, I've acquired a more discerning palate. *(sips his wine)* This really is really rather good.

HARVEY: *(HARVEY samples his wine and examines the label on the bottle)* Excellent, perfectly chilled.

BASIL: I have a great idea.

HARVEY: What a rarity that is.

BASIL: Do you remember? About a year ago, your magazine published an article about an alcoholic in America?
HARVEY: Never saw it.

BASIL: Bill something... Wilson, that was it! Evidently, he sets up meetings with fellow alcoholics to discuss the reasons for their addiction... he calls it Alcoholics Anonymous.

HARVEY: Alcoholics having anonymous meetings to discuss the merits of alcohol? Sounds fun to me... maybe I should join?

BASIL: No, it's no fun, on the contrary. They meet to talk about the reasons for their addiction, in an attempt to stop drinking.

HARVEY: Ah, now that sounds boring.

BASIL: It occurred to me, you could volunteer your servic es.

HARVEY: My services?

BASIL: Modelling your silk polka dot boxers. That image alone, would cure anyone's addiction to any alcohol, let alone brown ale. (laughs)

HARVEY: You should be grateful. After all, I did you a favour. You needed to get rid of those ghastly working class habits of yours.

BASIL: Dear old Harvey, such a snob. Remember, some of us are not privileged enough to be the second son of an Earl. Besides, I'm not ashamed of my roots. On the contrary, I'm very proud of them. True, nowadays, I do prefer a decent glass of wine to a brown ale. But it doesn't mean I'm ashamed of where I come from. My dad, a bank teller and my mum, working in a shop... nothing wrong with that.

HARVEY: I wasn't suggesting there was.

BASIL: Nevertheless, the inference was there.

HARVEY: Well, it wasn't intended to be. Going to a church school, getting into a grammar school, then a scholarship to Cambridge. I take my hat off to you, I really do.

BASIL: So you say, but at times, you can be so bloody patronising.

HARVEY: Don't blame me. That's what an Etonian education does for you. After all, if God were an Englishman, without doubt, he would be an old Etonian. Anyway you know I'm no snob.

BASIL: *(laughs)* Of course not!

HARVEY: Yes, true. I did have a privileged childhood and an excellent education. But I barely scraped through my exams on English literature. I struggled even more with modern history... and after all that effort, what have I achieved from it? Nothing.

BASIL: Ah, now you're just fishing for compliments.

HARVEY: Okay, well next to nothing then. *(HARVEY tops up their glasses)*

BASIL: You have no reason to feel sorry for yourself. After all, you achieved what you wanted. You got your degrees and became an editor, of one of England's most popular magazines. Also, a fully fledged journalist taboot.

HARVEY: Yes, sure, it sounds good on paper. But I only got the job, because my father was a friend of Lord Rothermere. Even then, they were hard pushed to find a position for me.

BASIL: Well lucky you, you fell on your feet. What a great job, getting all these freebie junkets around Europe.

HARVEY: Yes, *(whispers)* as the editor of the cooking section. Not exactly journalism is it?

BASIL: Don't be so hard on yourself. Be honest, you and the other bright young things, did party your way through university, and yet you still graduated. Whereas, I had my nose to the grindstone day and night to get a Master's in classics... and where did I end up? Working in a second hand bookshop on the Charing Cross road.

HARVEY: Be grateful, at least it's not a library, where you'd have to wander around whispering all day. *(the RECEPTIONIST interrupts)*

RECEPTIONIST: Ihre Schlüssel!

HARVEY: At last, our keys.

RECEPTIONIST: Gentleman, here are your keys, rooms 42 and 43, on the second floor. You have washing facilities in your rooms and the bathroom and toilet are on the same floor. Also both rooms are front facing, so have good views of the square.

HARVEY: Excellent, is there a lift?

RECEPTIONIST: *(RECEPTIONIST sarcastically)* Nein, but we have perfectly good stairs.

HARVEY: Yes, I see. Well then, would you be kind enough to get someone to carry our luggage up those perfect stairs, and to take them to our rooms?

RECEPTIONIST: Yes of course I will attend to it myself.

HARVEY: Thank you. *(HARVEY points to BASIL)* My friend would normally do it, but he appears to be exhausted from the journey. *(the RECEPTIONIST looks over at BASIL relaxing in the chair)* After some refreshment, he will no doubt rally. Then we can continue our journey, up your very elegant staircase, and see what excitement awaits us, on your second floor. *(the RECEPTIONIST grunts as he picks up the bags)*

BASIL: Thank heaven, you booked separate rooms, (BASIL laughs) at least I can lock my door.

HARVEY: *(HARVEY grins)* As you know, I've never been into warmed up soup.

BASIL: I'll take that as a compliment.

HARVEY: Looking back, I have to admit there was a brief moment in time, I had a crush on you. *(BASIL looks surprised)* But then, monogamy has always been too close in the dictionary, to monotony for my liking. At least after that alcoholic escapade, no matter how abhorrent and unmemorable for you. For me, that box was ticked. After all, I did get to sleep with you.

BASIL: *(sarcastically)* I am so pleased for you.

HARVEY: If only in the literal sense of the word. And even that's not true, I didn't get a wink of sleep, you snore appallingly.
BASIL: Must have been the drink.

HARVEY: But you did look cute. Innocently snoring away, unaware of whose bed you were really in. *(laughs)*

BASIL: If I didn't know you better, I'd swear you were showing a rare sign of sentiment.

HARVEY: Ah, but you do know me better, old darling.

BASIL: I do believe somewhere, hiding under that charming, but unbelievably cynical facade that you project, there is a sentimental old queen screaming to get out.

HARVEY: Less of the old, old boy. After all, I'm only a year older than you. *(pauses)* Oh dear, come to think of it, in October, I'll be a whole decade older.

BASIL: That's somewhat of an exaggeratIon... you'll be just one year older.

HARVEY: But I won't feel it. I'll be in my thirties and you'll still be in your twenties.

BASIL: Cheer up, it'll only be for one year. Then we will both be in our thirties. So, while we are still in our twenties, let's relax, finish this bottle and when it's a dead soldier, make our way up to our rooms and freshen up, ready for a night on the town.

HARVEY: Excellent idea! *(as HARVEY picks up the bottle, he looks over to the reception desk)* If Herr Smiler doesn't find our tickets. We'll have to drown our sorrows in this stuff and create, a whole case of dead soldiers. *(HARVEY tops up their drinks and drops the bottle back into the ice bucket)* Because let's face it, we won't have any reason to get up tomorrow morning.

BASIL: *(BASIL looks over at the RECEPTIONIST)* He seems a miserable old bugger… no humour.

HARVEY: He's alright, I'm sure. He's just a bit flustered with the confusion over our booking… and now this drama with our tickets.

BASIL: Looking around this place, it's news to me, any of them have humour.

HARVEY: Not quite fair, old man. Don't judge the whole German race by this small tacky hotel lobby. The Germans have a great sense of humour. Well they certainly did when I was here last. Not quite the same as ours of course, but nevertheless, take it from me, they do.

BASIL: *(sarcastically)* Then I'll just have to bow to your expert knowledge on the subject.

HARVEY: I will admit, Germany was so much more fun before this new Chancellor arrived.

BASIL: What's he got to do with the price of eggs?

HARVEY: Well, he is an Austrian after all. And who started the war to end all wars? Austrians.

BASIL: The Kaiser was to blame for that nightmare.

HARVEY: No, Austria invading Serbia, remember? That's when the whole caboodle kicked off.

BASIL: Technically, I suppose.

HARVEY: If it ever comes down to it. I wouldn't be surprised if the Austrians, make better Nazis than soldiers and the Germans better soldiers.

BASIL: With all that marching and goose stepping. That's probably the reason they don't have any humour... sore feet! *(BASIL chuckles)*

HARVEY: *(smiles)* Trust me, they certainly do. You just have to know how to tap into it.

BASIL: I wouldn't bet on it.

HARVEY: Oh, I would. In fact, I'll wager you a good vintage champagne on it... No hold on, that'll be well out of your budget. Okay, instead, I'll wager you another bottle of this delicious German wine.

BASIL: If it's not too expensive, then you're on.

HARVEY: German, it is then. *(HARVEY takes another sip)* You have to admit, now it's properly chilled. It's delicious... and definitely not expensive, even for you.

BASIL: *(looks around)* Now how to prove you wrong?

HARVEY: I'll give it some thought.

BASIL: You don't have to. Look over there. *(BASIL looks over at the RECEPTIONIST)* For a start, see if you can make that miserable old bugger laugh.

HARVEY: Mmm, now that is rather a challenge... Well, here goes. *(HARVEY waves to the RECEPTIONIST to get his attention. The*

RECEPTIONIST comes over)

RECEPTIONIST: Mein Herr?

HARVEY: Would you be kind enough, to chill more of your delicious wine, for later?

RECEPTIONIST: Ja, natürlich, of course!

HARVEY: Oh just one last thing. Maybe there is something you could help me with?

RECEPTIONIST: Ja?

HARVEY: My friend here, is labouring under the misapprehension that German people do not have a sense of humour.

RECEPTIONIST: *(in German)* Was? *(the RECEPTIONIST frowns. HARVEY realises he has upset him and so quickly tries to backtrack)*

HARVEY: Of course, naturally, I don't agree with him. It's just that, this is his first time in your wonderful country. Unlike myself of course. I know only too well, Germans have a wonderful sense of humour. *(RECEPTIONIST nods in agreement)* But then I've been coming here for many years. *(the RECEPTIONIST shows vague signs of a smile)* I spent nearly a year in Berlin studying. And I have to say, it's such a great night life! *(HARVEY winks)*

RECEPTIONIST: Diese schmutzigen Saupreußen. Degenerates!

HARVEY: Oops! Yes, you are so right, these damn Prussians are degenerates. *(HARVEY whispers to BASIL)* Thankfully I have had many a first hand experience to know that's true. *(HARVEY looks back to the RECEPTIONIST)* Anway please forgive my friend's impertinence but as I said, it is his first time here. And it's just his impression, not mine.

RECEPTIONIST: Then he is a Dummkopf! *(RECEPTIONIST chuckles)* Of course we Germans have a great sense of humour! We love to laugh and enjoy a joke like anybody else.

HARVEY: Jolly good. I agree.

BASIL: *(BASIL whispers to HARVEY)* Agreeing with him proves nothing. Make him laugh!

HARVEY: Patience old darling. *(HARVEY looks back to the receptionist)* Talking of humour, I heard a very funny joke coming here on the plane this morning. Would you care to hear it?

RECEPTIONIST: Ja, why not?

HARVEY: Well, it went like this. Your Fuhrer, the wonderful Herr Hitler, was recently doing some charity work. He was visiting a lunatic asylum. As he walked around the wards, everybody saluted him, except for one man. When he asked why he wasn't saluting. The man replied, 'well, I'm the hospital psychiatrist, so I'm the only sane person here!' *(The RECEPTIONIST frowns and in silence he walks away. HARVEY calls after him)* Sorry about that. You will still chase up our tickets for tomorrow's games?

RECEPTIONIST: Ja, ja. *(RECEPTIONIST walks back behind the reception desk and off stage)*

BASIL: As I said, no humour! *(BASIL chuckles)* It appears the wine is on you old boy.

HARVEY: Well, I suppose these days, it's more a question of whom, rather than what they are allowed to laugh about. Hope when he finds our tickets, he doesn't destroy them.

BASIL: Am sure he wouldn't do that, but he certainly wasn't amused. Far from it. You should be more careful, Harvey. You could get us into trouble.

HARVEY: *(suddenly from off stage coming from the RECEPTIONIST we hear a raucous belly laugh. HARVEY grins)* Oops! Sorry Basil, it appears the wine is on you, old bean!

BASIL: *(tuts)* Fair enough.

HARVEY: *(HARVEY gets up and walks over to the hotel window and looks out onto the square outside)* My goodness, look out there. This town is seething with beauty of all kinds. Come see for yourself.

BASIL: Why? What am I missing? *(BASIL joins him at the window and they both peer out)*

HARVEY: *(HARVEY gets quite excited)* Just look out there. Look at the crowds gathering, all drawn to Berlin, just to soak up the atmosphere before for the games tomorrow. Can't you just feel it? This town is literally pulsating with anticipation. It's just throbbing with sex.

BASIL: Sorry, can't say I do old man. I don't suffer from your particular form of tunnel vision, where everything seems to focus on sex. Behave yourself, you're getting too loud. From what I hear, it is also crawling with secret police, pickpockets and informers. Remember you are meant to be an affiliated journalist, covering the games. So at least, try to look the part, be more discreet.

HARVEY: Yes, yes, I know. But you have to admit, have you ever seen so many sexy people, crammed into one place? Pinch me, in fact punch me, I think I've just died and gone to heaven.

BASIL: Don't tempt me.

HARVEY: Look at all those cute soldiers, not to mention those two sailors in their tight little bum freezer uniforms. There really is something for everyone.

BASIL: Not for me.

HARVEY: Yes, even for you. Look at those big busty blonde frauleins serving the beer. They are literally bursting out of those tight uniforms.

BASIL: They certainly are, but busting out in all the wrong places.

HARVEY: There's just no pleasing you. We are here to have some fun... you do remember fun? *(BASIL still looks serious)* And you have the cheek to accuse this lot of not laughing. What is the matter with you?

BASIL: Yes, of course we are. But it won't be much fun, if instead, we find ourselves arrested and spending our entire visit in a police cell. So just calm down and don't draw attention to us. Come on let's go back and sit down. *(they go back and sit down in the chairs)*

HARVEY: *(HARVEY tops up their glasses)* Yes, we both know that's the official reason for us being here. Yet you know and I know, the extent of my journalist skills, is to write down the contents of someone else's recipe. Rearrange them a little, then publish them as my own. Which is technically editing, but more aptly known as plagiarism

BASIL: You mean stealing.

HARVEY: Bit harsh old love. I wouldn't put it as crudely as that. It's not easy coming up with a great new dish of the month. Month on month, year after year.

BASIL: Well you have to admit, *(laughs)* it's ironic, especially as you can't cook.

HARVEY: Not quite true. Remember, that freebie weekend to Devon? Supposedly to cover the delights of Torquay? We thought the Tourist Board would check us into the Grand Hotel, but instead they dumped us in that godforsaken cottage in the middle of nowhere. On that trip, I cooked a full English breakfast more than once.

BASIL: You mean you burnt a full English, more than twice. Your version of an English breakfast, was to present something on a plate that was completely unrecognisable, and worse, inedible.

HARVEY: Well, it was you who chose the ingredients.

BASIL: Yes guilty! But what they actually were, after you'd cooked them, was anybody's guess.
HARVEY: *(HARVEY looks at the clock above the reception desk)* Blast! Look at the time. It's getting late... where are those tickets?

BASIL: They are an hour ahead here, don't forget.

HARVEY: Exactly, so I doubt they'll turn up now and it'll be too late in the morning. We have to be at the stadium at the crack of dawn. Otherwise, we'll miss the opening ceremony. That's all I came to see. Not all that sporting nonsense.

BASIL: But that's what it's about.

HARVEY: Maybe for you. I've never cared much for sport. Mind you, I have to admit. There is nothing better on a warm summer's day, than sitting in a deckchair on a village green, sipping a large Pimm's whilst watching a cricket match.

BASIL: True.

HARVEY: The still air of summer broken only by the sound of a leather ball hitting the hard willow bat of the batsman. Not to mention, watching all those cute young men running around in their cricket whites. It is all so delightfully British.

BASIL: *(scoffs)* And so delightfully embellished! Come off it. Whenever I've been with you to watch a game of cricket, you never once saw a match even halfway through. The only thing you saw were a couple of jugs of Pimm's. Before you spent the rest of the match, fast asleep in your deckchair. As for the still air? It was only broken by the sound of you snoring.

HARVEY: Well, can you blame me? It would be an understatement to say cricket can drag on. Professional matches go on for days. Thinking about it, I prefer a good opera or a concert. Much more civilised. *(HARVEY picks up one of the magazines on the table and flips through it)* No good to you, it's all in German.

BASIL: That's okay, I can get the gist of it.

HARVEY: *(HARVEY glances down at his watch)* Well, I'm sorry old boy. Seems I've dragged you here all for nothing. Doesn't look like the tickets will come now, it's well past office hours.

BASIL: That's alright, it's not your fault, it's out of your hands. Look at the good side, we're in Berlin and you love Berlin. Now we have a couple of days free to explore it, so let's instead, just treat it as a holiday.

HARVEY: Appears we have little choice. But I really wanted to go. I was going to have a serious stab at writing about the opening and describe the whole atmosphere of the place. All going well, the magazine may have published it. Who knows, I could even have gotten myself promoted out of the cookery section and become a proper journalist.

BASIL: Am sorry matey, I really am.

VON GANTZ: *(at that moment off stage is the distant sound of jackboots. An elegant, middle aged man, smartly dressed in civilian clothes, enters from the hotel entrance, followed by an SS man. As he goes over to the reception desk, the RECEPTIONIST does a Hitler salute)* Heil Hitler!

BASIL: Bloody hell Harvey. He's full of himself.

HARVEY: He has reason to be. *(HARVEY discreetly points to the photo on the front of the magazine)* He's the Deputy Sports Minister. Don't stare, but if he looks over... smile! After all he's just the man we need to see. How's your German?

BASIL: As you know, at best very rusty at worst, non-existent.

HARVEY: *(HARVEY checks the magazine)* Count Siegfried von Gantz. Well wish me luck, it seems I'm in need of a word with our dear Count.

BASIL: Are you mad? He looks far too important, he's even got a body guard.

HARVEY: I'm not exactly unimportant myself. Remember I too have connections. Maybe it's time I used them. After all, on this occasion, a little snobbery mixed with a touch of name - dropping might not hurt. It might even help. *(HARVEY walks over to VON GANTZ who has his back to him, talking to the RECEPTIONIST. As HARVEY approaches, the SS bodyguard clicks his heels and stands at attention. HARVEY looks at VON GANTZ, who seems to be settling a bill)*

VON GANTZ: *(as VON GANTZ turns around, he looks surprised to see HARVEY standing behind him. He looks him up and down. Does a Hitler salute and grins)* Sind Sie Engländer.

HARVEY: *(HARVEY does a half hearted salute)* Ja, ich bin Engländer, Journalist.

VON GANTZ: Then speak English. *(looks at his bodyguard, then grins)* We Germans can master the English very easily... The language that is.

HARVEY: How did you know I was English?

VON GANTZ: The cut of your suit. A good English tailor stands out anywhere in the world.

HARVEY: Well thank you. I'll be sure to tell Mr Moses, my English tailor in Savile Row.

VON GANTZ: *(VON GANTZ is not amused)* Yes well, Jews can be very good at that sort of thing. All that banking and tailoring, about sums them up.

HARVEY: Not forgetting science and music of course. And you have to admit. There's nothing more relaxing, than sipping a good whisky, whilst listening to Mahler's symphony number five.

VON GANTZ: Sounds very cosy indeed, but then I will have to bow to your better knowledge of Jewish composers. I prefer the great German composers, Bach, Beethoven and of course the great man himself, Wagner! Even as an Englishman, you must concede Richard Wagner is the greatest of all composers.

HARVEY: Lohengrin, Das Rheingold, Tannhäuser and of course the Ride of the Valkyries… yes he certainly is a great composer. But the greatest? I would say that's down to one's personal taste. Wouldn't you? *(HARVEY realises VON GANTZ isn't amused)* To be fair, I do find Wagner spellbinding, if at times a little sinister. But I also like your other great German composers, you have so many talented ones.

VON GANTZ: *(nods in agreement)* Yes, of course we do.

HARVEY: It's amazing, just thinking about it. Beethoven, Bach, Brahms. Then there is Schumann, not to mention. Handel. It's true, the list of German composers is endless.

VON GANTZ: *(again nods in agreement and then smiles)* And as you say, all of them German… and all of them great.

HARVEY: Not forgetting of course, the other great composers. And as far as the Italian's where would one begin? Verdi? Puccini?

VON GANTZ: Yes... but too many Arias and all that bel canto nonsense.

HARVEY: You can't argue with beautiful singing, surely?

VON GANTZ: Of course, if it is too sentimental.

HARVEY: Tchaikovsky. For me personally, he's the greatest of all romantic composers. His ballet compositions are, as you know, numerous.

VON GANTZ: Yes, and they are all for women. They are not manly!

HARVEY: Surely not? You have to concede, there is nothing more masculine than his 1812 overture. Slowly building to a grand finale. But one, unlike any other... boom! The sound of cannon fire. I would have thought being German, you would appreciate the climax.

VON GANTZ: Too Russian for my liking. As you English would say. He's not my cup of tea. Or my shot of vodka! *(laughs)* Give me a Snapps anytime. All those ridiculous ballets. *(raises his eyebrows)* Grown men prancing about like tarts. No, it's not normal, not masculine. Give me a good German opera anytime.

HARVEY: Like you, I'm also rather fond of composers closer to home. For me it's our own dear Elgar.

VON GANTZ: Ja, ja. Edward Elgar. Typically British. All pomp and circumstance. But no real substance, mere jingoism. Land of Hope and Glory. He lived in the past. When Britain had real power. *(VON GANTZ stands closer to HARVEY)* Now then, the Honourable Harvey Cecil- Miller, I'm sure you didn't walk over here to debate the merits of our mutual composers. Even if you are the second son of the Earl of Keswick.

HARVEY: I see you too have done your homework.

VON GANTZ: I checked the register.

HARVEY: And you are Count von Gantz, Deputy Minister of Sport.

VON GANTZ: I see you also have done your homework.

HARVEY: To be perfectly honest, I read it in that magazine over there.

VON GANTZ: It seems the magazine is correct. Except in our new Germany, we have dispensed with the formality of titles. I know in England you treasure your outdated class system, but in Germany it makes little impression. Of course my own title, having been in my family for centuries, it's not so easy to discard, especially on my estate. Luckily for me, tenants are slow to change the old ways.

HARVEY: As you are the Deputy Minister of Sport, I wondered...

VON GANTZ: *(VON GANTZ interrupts)* Enough! Before you ask, I am far too busy to give interviews. You must appreciate, tomorrow is a very special day for us Germans. For the whole world in fact. Tomorrow, you are going to witness the greatest games ever staged.

HARVEY: Yes I know, and you are right. I didn't come over to you to speak about the merits of classical composers, or to seek an interview. Yes, I am a journalist... but it's not an interview I'm seeking.

VON GANTZ: *(As VON GANTZ goes to leave, he turns back)* Out of interest, if you didn't want an interview, what did you want?

HARVEY: I'm here to cover the games, but our tickets and passes from the Ministry haven't yet arrived. They were meant to be here when we checked in. But so far nothing has come.

VON GANTZ: *(VON GANTZ looks over at BASIL. BASIL smiles back)* What is your travelling companion's name?

HARVEY: Basil Hopkins, he was up at Cambridge with me.

VON GANTZ: *(VON GANTZ goes behind the reception desk to talk to the RECEPTIONIST. VON GANTZ then turns back to HARVEY)* You are rather slumming it, staying here aren't you?

HARVEY: I had no choice. My assignment was last minute and it appears every hotel in Berlin has been fully booked for months. I suppose that's the reason you are staying here? I would have thought you would have been able to get in anywhere.

VON GANTZ: *(roars with laughter)* I'm not staying here! *(VON GANTZ puts his arm on HARVEY'S shoulder and pulls him to one side)* I can see we are both men of the world. *(looks over at BASIL)* It seems, with very different tastes. It is true, I do have rooms booked here, but never for the night. Just for the odd hour or so.

HARVEY: Don't you find it odd? There seems to be very few staff. *(HARVEY points to the RECEPTIONIST)* He's the only one I've seen so far.

VON GANTZ: There is a cook and a chambermaid somewhere. His wife died a few years ago. So he now runs the place practically single handed. The hotel is usually empty. Which suits me. More discrete, *(VON GANTZ taps his nose)* if you catch my meaning.

HARVEY: Of course, I understand completely, mum's the word. I'm sorry for bothering you with this ticket business. It must seem a trivial matter, but for me, it's my career on the line.

VON GANTZ: No, not all! Far from it. When I find out who is responsible. It will be their career on the line, not yours. After all, anything that concerns my Ministry is never a trivial matter. I pride myself on being organised, and if somebody in any department is lazy, or inefficient, I want to be first to know... and they will pay for it. After all, it reflects on the whole Ministry

HARVEY: I really am sorry about this.

VON GANTZ: Don't be, my smart little Englishman. After all, it is not your fault. But have no doubt, I will find out who is responsible and they will be punished accordingly. Be reassured, coming straight to me, you did the right thing. And as a gentleman and fellow aristocrat. I give you my word, I will handle this personally. It will be sorted out by morning and, as you English say, heads will roll.

HARVEY: I think that's probably more of a French thing.

VON GANTZ: Even so, relax and have a pleasant stay in our Fatherland. Go out tonight, enjoy this beautiful city. I'm sure you'll find plenty of things to do. I'll have your tickets sent over before you return.

HARVEY: Splendid, Count. I am very grateful to you. By way of returning your hospitality, if you are ever back in England, do come and visit Burghley Hall, our little pile in the country.

VON GANTZ: Yes I know of it, I'm told it's quite charming.

HARVEY: Well depending on the time of year, we could bag a few pheasants. Also our neighbours on the next estate, host a jolly good fox hunt.

VON GANTZ: Ja, Farley Hall. I know the owner Lord Ragstone, very well. I've hunted there a couple of times, but that was at least ten years ago.

HARVEY: Then that was before I went up to Cambridge. Who knows we may have even ridden in the same hunt.

VON GANTZ: Quite possibly, what a small world it is. As you say, if ever I'm back in England, I will indeed take up your invite. You being a journalist, off the record, us aristocrats have to stick together ja? After all, it seems we are a dying breed.

HARVEY: Yes, I suppose we are.

VON GANTZ: Well, as enjoyable as this brief encounter has been, time marches on and duty calls. (*goes to leave, then turns back*) Ah, if you do change your mind about not wanting to interview me, contact my office after the opening tomorrow. Who knows it could be fun for both of us.

HARVEY: Yes, I certainly will. Again, thank you

VON GANTZ: *(VON GANTZ hands HARVEY a card)* Here is my direct line. Keep it safe.

HARVEY: Yes, yes of course I will.

VON GANTZ: Heil Hitler! *(VON GANTZ clicks his heels, does a Hitler salute and walks out of the hotel followed by his bodyguard. HARVEY does another weak impersonation of a salute, then walks back over to BASIL, who is still sitting in the chair)*

BASIL: Well, that was one pompous, puffed up kraut! What was all that saluting business?

HARVEY: A means to an end old boy. I did it.

BASIL: I know, I saw you raise your arm... disgraceful!

HARVEY: Not that, I mean I did it.

BASIL: Did what exactly?

HARVEY: Got the tickets old darling! And that's not all. He's promised me an exclusive interview!

BASIL: Wow! I take my hat off to you Harvey. You have more front than all the windows at Selfridges. How did you manage to pull it off?
HARVEY: Our mutual love of music, combined with my irresistible charm of course... And my family title didn't hurt either.

BASIL: But how are you going to slip him into your cookery page? Hitler's favourite Rhineland soup perhaps? Let's face it, he guzzled that up quick enough.

HARVEY: Do stop your nonsense! As you said yourself, you never know who is earwigging. Anyway, that's not funny... it's just vulgar.

BASIL: Ah come on, vulgar? What's vulgar about that?

HARVEY: The Rhineland was German after all. I think that's why Hitler's such a hero to them. That Versailles Treaty business. I wouldn't be surprised, if it comes back to bite us.

BASIL: Hopefully right on your arse.

HARVEY: What do they say? Can you take them out of where?

BASIL: I know all too well, where... Croydon. And as it happens, I took myself out and I'm proud of that fact. I'm not ashamed of Croydon, it can be very nice as it happens. Not that you would have an inkling, having never ever been south of the river. It's a place where normal people live, in normal sized houses. Ones built for ordinary families. Not grand ornate museum pieces, designed to show off the family's power.

HARVEY: Nothing wrong with a bit of power old dear.

BASIL: Listen to yourself. Before we leave here, you'll be volunteering for the Hitler Youth.
HARVEY: Certainly not, I look ghastly in shorts. Knobbly knees, you see.

BASIL: I'd rather not see. And for what it's worth, I still don't see how von Gantz is going to fit into your cookery slot.

HARVEY: That's easy. He's not going to. No, I'm going to use this opportunity to do an exclusive interview about his homelife, his country estate. Why he became a National Socialist. More importantly, the inside story of the Olympic Games and his vision on Germany's future. Then I'm going to tie it all up together, and when it's written, I'll dump it on my editor's desk. And if he won't use it, plenty of other magazines will. This is the breakthrough I've been looking for. My big chance. You just wait, Basil. If I get this one right, it really will be a scoop. And I'll be scooped up by Fleet Street in no time. At last, me, Harvey Cecil-Miller, a real journalist. Doing my very own features. Gosh, I'm so excited!

BASIL: Well, don't get too excited. Calm yourself, let's go and check out our rooms, unpack and freshen up. Then we can hit the town to celebrate.

HARVEY: Okay, but we'd best not over do it. Remember we're up early. *(they stand up. HARVEY surveys the room. As he does, two fit young men in naval uniform, in their mid twenties enter the lobby. They look around and head for the reception desk. One is very handsome, with blond hair, the other is average good looks with brown hair)* Oh my goodness, it's Christmas already! *(as BASIL goes to stand*

HARVEY pushes him back in his seat) Relax, let's not be too hasty!

BASIL: What?
HARVEY: Look over there! Those two sailors from the street. They are checking in. *(BASIL looks around to see what the fuss is about about)*

BASIL: Oh, no. I don't believe it.

HARVEY: Do believe it! *(the two sailors talk to the RECEPTION-*

IST) Look at that perfect specimen of Germanic manhood! *(the sailors seem disappointed and look around for somewhere to sit. HARVEY tries to catch the blond one's eye line. When he does, he beckons them over)*

BASIL: *(BASIL obviously embarrassed tries to stop him)* For God's sake Harvey, don't embarrass me, people are watching.

HARVEY: Watching what exactly? Let them watch. I'm only trying to help them. *(the two sailors walk over to HARVEY)* Gentleman, if you're looking for somewhere to sit, there are chairs over there by the window.

GÜNTER: Die Engländer, eh?

HARVEY: That's right old luvvie, got it in one.

GÜNTER: *(GÜNTER grins)* Sehr gern.

HARVEY: Wie sind Eure Namen?

GÜNTER: *(GÜNTER touches chest)* Ich bin Günter. *(GÜNTER points to his friend)* Das ist Hans.

BASIL: *(BASIL looks at HARVEY)* Just tell him, there are chairs over there and let them go.
HARVEY: *(HARVEY ignores BASIL)* Do you speak English Günter?

GÜNTER: Ja, I speak a little. Mein Freund nicht... not much.

HARVEY: You are staying in the hotel?

GÜNTER: Nein. We have been walking around the city all day, trying to find a preiswerte Zimmer.

HARVEY: Ah, an inexpensive room? *(HARVEY scoffs)* In Berlin the day before the Olympics? That's a tall order old darling. Everything has been booked solid for months, if not years. There is absolutely nothing. That's why we are in this off the beaten track flea pit. We had no choice, and even here it isn't cheap.

GÜNTER: Yes we know, for such a hotel, It is twice the price it should be. *(GÜNTER gestures toward the RECEPTIONIST)* He was not helpful.

HARVEY: Old Smiler, no he isn't.

GÜNTER: Old Smiler?

HARVEY: Our little nickname for him, as he never smiles. *(HANS seems puzzled)* Spitzname! *(GÜNTER explains to HANS and they both laugh)* Well. at least stay and have a drink and rest your weary feet, gentleman.

GÜNTER: Danke, but here the beer is also expensive, so we go to a little bar further down the road.

HARVEY: No, my treat! I wouldn't dream of letting you do that. You are my guests.

GÜNTER: *(GÜNTER confers with HANS and then answers)* Ja, well... danke for your kind offer. Then after, we have to go and look for a cheap zimmer..

HARVEY: Well I wouldn't bank on it, old darling. You won't find a room anywhere. We are practically in the suburbs as it is.

GÜNTER: If this is alright, we will join you for a drink.

HARVEY: Yes do, bring those chairs over. *(as GÜNTER and HANS turn to walk over to the chairs)* You like wine, yes?

GÜNTER: Nein. Bier, bitte.

HARVEY: Then beer it is. Beer to celebrate!

GÜNTER: Celebrate?

HARVEY: It's a long story, old darling. Anyway, the beer is on me.

HANS: *(GÜNTER speaks quietly to HANS in German. HANS looks at HARVEY suspiciously)* Ja, ja, sie sind queers, ja?

GÜNTER: Nein, einfach Englisch.

HANS: Freibier, eh? Das ist sehr gut.

HARVEY: *(HARVEY is listening to what they are saying and chuckles)* Yes, that is very good. Free beer from the queer. *(HARVEY gets up and goes over to the RECEPTIONIST)* Could you be a sport, and bring us over another bottle? Also two beers and some sandwiches. *(as HARVEY walks back to BASIL, he looks over at the RECEPTIONIST)* Oh, and I'll signal, if we need anything else. *(the RECEPTIONIST nods. GÜNTER and HANS bring over the chairs and sit down)* Ah, that's much better. *(HARVEY whispers to BASIL, as he looks at GÜNTER)* Perfect. If this is an example of the master race, he can master me any night.

BASIL: Steady on Harvey, he might report you.

HARVEY: Not a chance! Anyway, he didn't hear me, and even if he did, I spoke far too fast, for him to understand. *(HARVEY looks at GÜNTER)* Did you, my German beauty?

GÜNTER: *(in German)* Was?

HARVEY: Did you understand a word of what I said to my dear friend Basil here?

GÜNTER: Ja, ja... I think a little. *(GÜNTER smiles)*

HARVEY: *(HARVEY winks)* Oops! I had better be more careful what I whisper in future.

RECEPTIONIST: *(the RECEPTIONIST arrives with more wine and two stein mugs of beer, which he places on the table. He looks disapprovingly, as he notices HARVEY obviously letching over GÜNTER)* Next I will bring the sandwiches you ordered.

BASIL: You ordered sandwiches? But I thought we were going out?

HARVEY: Well, I see no reason to go out and get squashed in the crowd, when we are all so cozy here. Anyway we can do all that tomorrow. Remember it's an early start in the morning. *(HARVEY hands GÜNTER and HANS their beer and pours more wine for BASIL and himself)* So tell me Günter, where do you two hail from in Germany?

GÜNTER: Sorry?

Allan Warren

HARVEY: I don't mean hail. *(HARVEY jokingly raises his arm)* I mean, where do you come from.

GÜNTER: Ah, ja. Far from here. We both come from a little town outside Munich.

HARVEY: Well, you certainly came to the right place. *(GÜNTER doesn't react)* The Hotel Munich? As it says in the brochure, 'A taste of old Bavaria in the heart of Berlin'.

GÜNTER: *(GÜNTER smirks)* Nein, it is nothing like the Bavaria I come from, Garmisch Partenkirchen. It is in the mountains. It is clean and the air is so fresh, it is like minz on your breath.

HARVEY: Mmm, I bet it is. A mountain boy eh?

GÜNTER: *(GÜNTER: smiles)* No, a farmer's boy... We have a small farm down in the valley.

BASIL: Do you still live there?

GÜNTER: My father and my sister do *(GÜNTER looks at HANS)* We are billeted in Bremerhaven. But I go home to see my father when I get leave.

HARVEY: Your Father? Your parents don't live together?

GÜNTER: No, my mother died when I was young. She had, how do you say? Weak lungs... krebs.

HARVEY: Lung cancer? I'm very sorry to hear that. That's rough. My mother died of it too, it was while I was still at university.

47

BASIL: *(BASIL points at HARVEY and smirks)* He helped send her on her way

GÜNTER: *(in German)* Was? Ist das gut? Please, speak slowly.

HARVEY: No, it's just his stupid joke. *(HARVEY turns to BASIL)* Basil, do me a favour... never joke about my mother again, It's just not funny, besides, it's not true... Unlike my father, I loved my mother very much.

BASIL: Well at least you still have your father.

HARVEY: Now that is a joke. To him, I'm just the spare to his beloved heir. It's my brother that gets all his the attention, not me. Whereas, my mother loved us both equally.... I still miss her a lot.

BASIL: Maybe, but you have to admit, your little scandal did nothing to improve her health.

HARVEY: Me being sent down from Cambridge, had absolutely nothing to do with my mother's death. Anyway, they do say, being rusticated is a prerequisite for a good education.
BASIL: Not being caught being buggered by the Arts Master wasn't.

HARVEY: He did no such thing. He was just giving me a private lesson in watercolors.

BASIL: Oh, is that what you call it?

HARVEY: Yes... It was all very innocent. Just a little picnic by the river, as we painted. And being a particularly hot day, naturally we went skinny dipping. But when I tried to climb out, the river bank was far too steep, so he helped by pushing from behind.

BASIL: *(BASIL laughs)* Naked of course! No wonder you were caught.

HARVEY: It wasn't my fault, we were seen from the other bank.

BASIL: Half the university saw you.

HARVEY: Yes, and they even applauded. Anyway he saved my life.

BASIL: Then it's a pity you didn't try to save his career. After all, you lost him his job, even though it was you leading him on.

HARVEY: Well, he didn't have to take advantage of my generous nature did he? Stop being so tedious, you're boring these two handsomes lads. *(HARVEY smiles at GÜNTER)* Another beer?

GÜNTER: *(GÜNTER nods)* Ja, noch ein bier, bitte.

BASIL: Same old, Harvey. *(BASIL looks at GÜNTER)* Poor boy, leave him alone.

HARVEY: Ah, don't be fooled. He knows what my game is. Anyway you're drunk.

BASIL: I'm not anywhere near drunk.

HARVEY: You're half pissed at least, I'll top you up, then maybe you'll get really drunk and fall asleep and give us all a break. *(HARVEY looks back at GÜNTER and HANS)* Am so sorry if my friend is boring you with his jabbering.

GÜNTER: Was ist, jabbering? I don't understand.

HARVEY: Hmm, let me see... Geschwätz.

GÜNTER: Ah ja... No, please it is interesting. It is good for me to learn better English.

HARVEY: (HARVEY looks back at BASIL) Seems I owe you an apology, old boy.

BASIL: (BASIL raises his glass) Accepted! Now Send them on their way, stop being selfish and let's go out of here.

HARVEY: As you know, I've always been rich, I've always been spoilt and I've always been selfish! And what's more, I've always enjoyed all three in equal measure, so why on earth should I change?

BASIL: Why? Because who knows, you might even grow to like yourself.

HARVEY: (HARVEY ignores BASIL'S remark and turns to GÜNTER who is chatting to HANS) How old are you?

GÜNTER: Ich bin twenty four in April. I was born one day before our Fuhrer's birthday, so my family holds birthday celebrations for two days, not just one.

HARVEY: Twenty three and already in uniform, it's very becoming.

GÜNTER: Sorry? (GÜNTER looks down at his uniform)

HARVEY: Very smart.

GÜNTER: *GÜNTER proudly sits up and puts his hand on his chest)* Ja, very good, ja?

HARVEY: Yes indeed, very, very nice.

GÜNTER: Danke, But these days, nearly everybody in Germany has a uniform. Is it not so in England?

HARVEY: No, not so.

GÜNTER: Nein? But why?

HARVEY: In England, we don't have conscription. *(GÜNTER appears confused)* Wehrpflicht? Meaning people volunteer. It is not compulsory to join the armed forces.

GÜNTER: But a strong country needs people in uniform.

HARVEY: Hopefully not the British, our uniforms look far too coarse for my skin. *(GÜNTER doesn't appear to understand, so HARVEY scratches himself)* Itchy? Scratchy.

GÜNTER: Ah, Kratzig!
HARVEY: Yes, kratzig, my skin is very sensitive.

BASIL: Unlike his feelings.

HARVEY: Thank you Basil, *(HARVEY turns back to GÜNTER)* So do you come to Berlin often?

BASIL: *(BASIL chuckles)* D'you come to Berlin often? Sounds like you're about to ask him for a dance.

HARVEY: *(HARVEY signals the RECEPTIONIST for more drinks)* I'm merely making polite conversation, that's all.

BASIL: We all know what you're trying to make.

HARVEY: You are such a cynic. You know, I have a weakness for uniforms.

BASIL: You and the whole of Germany it seems.

HARVEY: *(the RECEPTIONIST arrives with more beer and wine and clears away the old mugs and bottles, then leaves)* Günter, have you ever been to England? It's beautiful at this time of year. *(before GÜNTER can answer)*

BASIL: Why don't you ask him about himself? No danger of you boring him that way. People love talking about themselves. Let's face it, with you it's been a lifetime obsession.

HARVEY: *(HARVEY leans over to GÜNTER)* Günter, what do you think of your Adolph Hitler?

BASIL: That does it! What's that saying about politics and religion?
HARVEY: Oh, do shut up. Besides, it's a good way to liven up even the dullest of dinner parties.

GÜNTER: *(GÜNTER seems nervous)* Er ist ein großartiger Kanzler. A good Chancellor

HARVEY: Yes, I agree, he seems to be a very good Chancellor, indeed.

GÜNTER: *(GÜNTER struggles with his English, so he speaks slowly)* I am thinking he has already done great things and will go on to do greater things.

HANS: Ja... he has taken back our Rhineland.

GÜNTER: This is true.

HANS: They say he will soon take back other German speaking land that was stolen from us. Then our country will be one Deutschland again.

BASIL: Oh dear, you have put the penny in the slot.

GÜNTER: He has made Deutsche stolz Deutsch zu sein. It is a good feeling

HARVEY: *(BASIL looks over at HARVEY for translation)* He is proud to be a German.

BASIL: And why not? But I wish you'd change the subject and...

HANS: *(HANS interrupts)* We are no longer subordinantes to foreigners or Jewish bankers. Now there is work for everybody.
BASIL: Wow! You've certainly woken this one up.

GÜNTER: Ja, it is true. Nobody goes hungry anymore. There is work and Lebensmittel, food for everybody.

BASIL: As they say, out of the mouths of babes!

HARVEY: I thought your friend didn't speak English?

GÜNTER: No, not very much. Just a few English words. My English too, ist nicht gut.

HARVEY: No it's very good. I had best watch my P's and Q's in future. Because when I'm talking, I never know what I'm saying.

GÜNTER: *(in German)* Was?

HARVEY: Just an observation. So tell me, were you in the Hitler Youth?

BASIL: I think we already know the answer to that.

GÜNTER: Ja, we were both in the Hitler Youth. From fourteen, until eighteen years old. Before we joined the Navy, I was a Scharführer, a squad leader. HANS was champion boxer of our troop. *(GÜNTER taps HANS's biceps. HANS puts up his fists and punches the air)*

HANS: Ja, Ich bin ein großartiger Boxer. *(HANS lands a punch on GÜNTER'S shoulder)*

GÜNTER: Ouch! *(GÜNTER obviously in pain, shrugs him off as he rubs his arm)* Hitler Youth, it is like your English Boy Scouts ja?

HARVEY: Sort of, but our Boy Scouts are not at all political.
GÜNTER: Political?

HARVEY: Not attached to any political party.

BASIL: Anyone can join, whatever their political or religious views.

GÜNTER: Anyone? This cannot be good.

HARVEY: Why not?

GÜNTER: How can you keep Disziplin? What if they are kommunistisch? And how would you know if every member ist echt Aryan?

HARVEY: Oh, we don't worry about things like that, old boy. Our scouts are far too busy, pitching tents, making campfires, or frying sausages and of course, doing good deeds.

GÜNTER: We do this also.

HARVEY: Not to mention doing good deeds.

BASIL: *(BASIL points to HARVEY)* Something he's avoided since birth, in case he gets punished.

GÜNTER: Sorry?
BASIL: You must know the saying? No good deed goes unpunshed...

HARVEY: Just ignore him. Now, I bet you don't salute with three fingers? Like this. *(HARVEY salutes with three fingers)*

GÜNTER: Drei Finger? Nein. Wir machen das *(GÜNTER sits up straight and does a Hitler salute)*

HARVEY: Oh, we don't have any of that Sieg Heil business, or all that standing to attention. I think we'd find raising ones arms far too exhausting. No, we just use three fingers, along with a lot of dib dobbing.

The Matching Pair - Part 1: No Good Deed

GÜNTER: Dib Dobbing? *(GÜNTER looks at HANS)*

HANS: Dib dobbing?

HARVEY: Oh, and dib dabbing!

BASIL: *(chuckles)* You shouldn't wind them up.

GÜNTER: Ah! You are making a joke, yes?

HARVEY: No, not at all. They are wonderful lyrics, meaningful. But meaning what? I have yet to fathom. *(HARVEY speaks the lyrics)* 'Ging gang, goolie, goolie, ging gang goo, ging gang goo.' Ah, that takes me back. I still have my neckerchief and toggle.

GÜNTER: *(laughs)* All this dibbing and dobbing and ging gang goolie. You English are definitely crazy.

HANS: In the Hitler Youth we had songs we could march to. Songs that mean something. (HANS stands up and starts singing the Hiyler Youth flag song. HANS taps *GÜNTER on the shoulder, to join him. GÜNTER seems reluctant but joins in)*

Vorwärts! Vorwärts! Schmettern die hellen Fanfaren,

Vorwärts! Vorwärts! Jugend kennt keine Gefahren,

Deutchland, du wirst Leuchtend stehn,

Mogen wir auch untergehn.

BASIL: *(as HANS and GÜNTER sing, BASIL turns to HARVEY)* You've certainly put the penny in the right slot there. Whatever it is they're singing about, they are getting very loud.

HANS & GÜNTER: Vorwärts! Vorwärts! Schmettern die hellen

Fanfaren, Vorwärts! Vorwärts! Jugend kennt keine Gefahren,
St das Ziel auch noch so hoch,
Jugend zwingt es doch!

HARVEY: (HANS and GÜNTER continue singing) It's something about going forward, under the blare of bright fanfares and youth knowing no danger... Oh, and their flags flutters ahead of them. (HANS and GÜNTER sing even louder) Right I've had enough of this nonsense! Come on Basil, let's give them a flutter of our flag... we can't let the side down, after all we are British. On the count of one, Ging Gang Goolie. (HARVEY stands up. BASIL at first looks embarrassed, then joins him. They do the boy scout salute and start to sing)

Ging gang, goolie, goolie,
ging gang goo, ging gang goo.
Ging gang, goolie goolie,
ging gang goo.

(HANS and GÜNTER seem surprised but continue singing. Then give up and collapse back in their chairs, laughing at BASIL and HARVEY. Unperturbed. HARVEY and BASIL continue)

Ging gang, goolie goolie,
goolie watcha, ging gang goo.
Ging gang goo...

RECEPTIONIST: (the RECEPTIONIST rushes over and interrupts) Gentleman, gentleman, please... not so loud, you are disturbing my other guests. Please stop this!

HARVEY: *(HARVEY and BASIL stop singing)* Oh dear, and we were just getting into our stride. Sorry, old boy. *(the RECEPTIONIST walks away shaking his head)*

HANS: *(HANS is still laughing)* If you call that mull... that garbage, a good marching song. You English really are mad.

BASIL: Not as mad as you Germans, with all that marching and strutting about like demented geese.

HARVEY: Well, to be fair, ours is more of a strolling, rather than a marching sort of song.

GÜNTER: *(GÜNTER doesn't look amused)* I think we should go now, we have drunk too much.

HARVEY: Nonsense, you've only had a couple of beers. Come on, eat some more of those sandwiches, they'll act like blotting paper. In the meantime I'll order us another round.

HANS: *(HANS whispers something to GÜNTER)* Er zahlt, ja?

GÜNTER: Ja.

HARVEY: *(HARVEY overhears)* Tell him to relax, of course I'm paying, old darling. After all, I invited you to sit with us.

GÜNTER: Sorry, he was not meaning to be rude.

HARVEY: Neither was my friend, he also is just a little tipsy. Anyway, I'm sure you can't afford what they charge in this dump. *(HARVEY looks in the direction of the RECEPTIONIST)* Old Smiler over there has obviously bumped up the prices because of the games.

GÜNTER: We leave now, yes?

BASIL: If you ask me, old ducks, they have cottoned onto what your game is.

HARVEY: *(to BASIL)* You can be so negative. *(HARVEY looks back at GÜNTER)* Leave now? No, don't be silly, stay for one more drink. Can't have you accusing me of being mean.

GÜNTER: Mean? Was ist mean?

HARVEY: Mean? Well I mean. Mean... you know? Miserly. *(HARVEY pulls out his wallet, puts it close to his face and starts counting his money. GÜNTER doesn't react)* Oh, what is it in German?

HANS: *(HANS laughs)* Jew! *(GÜNTER seems embarrassed. HANS nudges him with his elbow. Reluctantly GÜNTER smiles)*

HARVEY: No, no... *(HARVEY does his impersonation again)*

GÜNTER: *(GÜNTER whispers something to HANS who replies in German)* Ah, geizig!

HARVEY: Yes, that's it, stingy. Well we can't have that can we?

GÜNTER: Nein, but...
HARVEY: *(HARVEY interrupts)* Then we are agreed, gentleman. *(HARVEY signals for more drinks)* Günter do you and your friend like music?

GÜNTER: *(GÜNTER confers with HANS)* Yes we do, very much.

BASIL: Let me guess? You like Wagner and military bands?
59

GÜNTER: Ja, of course, who does not?

BASIL: Me for a start.

HARVEY: *(HARVEY looks back at GÜNTER and HANS)* Military bands eh? Well that's understandable, you are in the armed forces. No what I meant was, do you like jazz?

HANS: No! In Germany, it is not considered music.

HARVEY: Well, that's one way of putting it. I certainly wouldn't describe it like that.

BASIL: *(BASIL looks at HANS)* Disgusting!

HANS: *(in German)* Was?

HARVEY: *(HARVEY to BASIL)* Pipe down and drink your wine. *(HARVEY jumps in before BASIL can explain)* He doesn't like his wine.

GÜNTER: Ja, I don't like wine either. *(GÜNTER leans in toward HARVEY, puts his finger to his lips, nudges HARVEY and grins)* But I like jazz. It is not banned in Germany. But it is considered not German... so many Germans do not play it.
BASIL: But, surely, outside of a national anthem, music belongs to every nationality? Whatever its origins. Either way, jazz is great music.

HARVEY: *(at that moment the RECEPTIONIST serves another round of drinks. This time he is smiling)* Bloody hell Basil, Herr Smiler is at last, living up to his nickname. Look he's actually smiling! *(the*

RECEPTIONIST leaves)

BASIL: Of course he is. This table's been groaning with drinks all evening, Your bar bill alone could pay to refurbish this dump.

HARVEY: *(HARVEY looks back at GÜNTER)* What about Cole Porter? You must have heard of him? You know *(HARVEY sings a couple of bars)*

You're the top, you're the colloseum
You're the top, you're the Louvre museum.

GÜNTER: *(HARVEY gets louder, so GÜNTER interrupts)* No sorry, I am not familiar with this. In my house, my father likes band music.

HARVEY: Me too. You like Glen Miller? *(GÜNTER doesn't react)* You know? *(HARVEY sings again)*
Pardon me boy, is this the Chattanooga choo, choo?
Track twenty nine'.
(HARVEY winks at GÜNTER) Boy you give me a shine...

GÜNTER: *(HANS gives a look of disapproval and GÜNTER becomes uncomfortable)* Please, not so loud! I don't like this.

BASIL: He's right for a change. Keep it down, old man. After all, you are tone deaf.

HARVEY: Sorry, it was the wine singing... Tell me Günter, have you two ever been out of Germany?

HANS: *(GÜNTER looks at HANS and says something in German)* When we finish our maneuvers, we will.

61

HARVEY: *(HARVEY sarcastically)* HANS, you're full of surprises. Your command of the English language is improving with every mugful of beer.

HANS: We have been to Gstaad, in German Switzerland.

HARVEY: I think you mean German - speaking Switzerland.

HANS: It is of little importance.

BASIL: *(BASIL mutters to himself)* Tell that to the Swiss.

GÜNTER: We have also been to Austria, but I suppose that also doesn't really count. I would like to travel somewhere far, like America and see New York and meet cowboys.

HARVEY: Shouldn't think you'll meet many in New York.

GÜNTER: Is it true they have buildings that are almost as tall as Wolken?

HARVEY: Wolken? Some maybe, even are higher than the clouds... Skyscrapers.

GÜNTER :   Ah, Wolkenkratzer? Mmmm, one day, I wish to go inside a skyscraper. It must be wonderful to be able to open a window and touch the clouds.

HARVEY: Not sure at that height, you'll be able to open a window. But The Empire State Building does have an observation deck.

GÜNTER: Yes, I have seen the Empire State in the Kino, when the Hindenburg flew over the whole city. For me, I don't think it will be possible to go there soon, but it is my dream.

HARVEY: Well, at least you can see it in the cinema.

GÜNTER: Yes, I go there as often as I can.

HARVEY: Me too. I just love it. That magical silver screen, ready to transport you anywhere you want to go.

GÜNTER: Es ist is magisch.

HARVEY: Yes, you're right, it is magical.

GÜNTER: So did you like America?

HARVEY: I have never been there.

BASIL: Just as well... they probably wouldn't let him in.

HARVEY: Thank you Basil. You really are too helpful. No I must confess, I haven't been to America. To be honest, I'm still fascinated by the real world... England.

HANS: England, the real world? Huh!

GÜNTER: Charlie Chaplin, he is English, yes?

HARVEY: Very much so, from south London.

HANS: He is funny no?

BASIL: Yes, rather like your Führer.

HANS: *(HANS and GÜNTER appear confused)* The Führer is not funny.

BASIL: Well at least, we're agreed on that. *(HANS looks at him suspiciously)*

HARVEY: He just means they look very similar.

HANS: Ähnich? They certainly do not!

HARVEY: Oh don't get all serious on me old darling. He just means their moustaches... You know *(HARVEY points to his upper lip)* moustaches!

GÜNTER: *(GÜNTER and HANS look at each other and smile)* Ah, ja. Schnurrbart... moustache!

HARVEY: Charlie Chaplin's latest film is called *Modern Times*. It came out about six months ago. Have you seen it?

HANS: Nein.

BASIL: It's a huge hit all over the world, I think it's fair to say, he is the greatest comedian of modern times.

HANS: Huh! That is nothing. Our Führer is the greatest leader of modern times. This Chaplin is just a comedian.

BASIL: So is your Herr Hit...

HARVEY: *(HARVEY nudges BASIL and quickly interrupts)* He's right about the film. It really is very funny.

HANS: I don't like funny films.

BASIL: *(BASIL sarcastically)* Why does that not surprise me?

HANS: This dummkopf comedian with the Schnurrbart. *(HANS touches his top lip)* He is just an actor in a film. I'm talking about a man who is influencing the whole of the modern world. Who will make Germany's dreams come true.

HARVEY: But Chaplin is also a purveyor of dreams.

HANS: Just fantasies, daydreams.

HARVEY: My point exactly. At least we agree on that. *(HARVEY sips some more wine)* cheers!

HANS: Sometimes you speak English too fast for me.

HARVEY: You do surprise me. Earlier you hardly spoke a word. You were just listening, taking it all in. Now, you're chatting away like a native Englishman.

HANS: We Germans are full of surprises.

HARVEY: *(HARVEY appears to be more than slightly drunk. He looks at GÜNTER and smiles at him)* Oh I just love surprises, especially big ones. *(GÜNTER turns away and starts chatting to HANS in German)*

BASIL: For God's sake Harvey. Pull yourself together! You're stripping him with your eyes.

HARVEY: Oh, don't throw a wobbly on me. At least it's not with my hands. After all, it's only a bit of fun.

BASIL: It's not fun for him, and it's embarrassing for me. I don't think it's funny. He obviously has no idea what your game is.

HARVEY: Of course he does. Well if he doesn't, he'll soon find out. *(HARVEY smiles at GÜNTER and pats his knee)*

GÜNTER: *(GÜNTER pushes his hand away)* Das ist nicht gut!. Stop this! *(GÜNTER takes his drink and beckons HANS to join him over near the window. Where they stand and talk out of earshot)*

BASIL: See what I mean? If you persist in chasing him, you're going to get us all into trouble. So just sober up. They're probably going to report you.

HARVEY: For what?

BASIL: For being a poof. I'm telling you, I smell trouble.

HARVEY: *(HARVEY ignores BASIL'S advice and leers at GÜNTER)* Huh! He's not going to make trouble. *(at that moment VON GANTZ'S SS body guard enters and heads straight toward HARVEY. As he does, GÜNTER and HANS tense up and stand to attention)*
BASIL :   That's torn it. I told you.

SS. MAN: *(SS MAN clicks his heels)* You are The Honourable Harvey Cecil-Miller?

HARVEY: Yes, but what of it? I haven't done anything.

SS.MAN: You haven't?

HARVEY: Nein. *(HARVEY appears worried and looks over at HANS and GÜNTER for support. HANS and GÜNTER quickly turn away and look out of the window)*

SS. MAN: You didn't ask for tickets? But the Deputy Sports Minister has arranged for your tickets for the opening of the games tomorrow.

HARVEY: *(HARVEY seems relieved)* Oh, sorry, yes of course.

SS. MAN: *The SS MAN clicks his heels and hands HARVEY the tickets)* With the compliments of Count von Gantz.

HARVEY: *(HARVEY smiles at the SS MAN)* Will you please thank the Count and tell him, he has my eternal gratitude. And also tell him what a great relief. *(HARVEY looks at BASIL)* In more ways the one.

SS.MAN: I will inform him of your message. *(SS MAN does a Hitler salute)* Heil Hitler! *(GÜNTER and HANS immediately stand to attention and, as the SS man goes to leave, in unison they salute)* Heil Hitler!

BASIL: Well I never, compliments of Count Von Gantz.
HARVEY: Too true, Basil, you never. You never do anything... useful that is. *(HARVEY signals the RECEPTIONIST for more drinks)*

BASIL: Never had your perpetual charm, old boy. Or your confidence.

HARVEY: You've been around me long enough, to learn at least one or the other. *(HARVEY kisses the tickets)*

RECEPTIONIST: *(the RECEPTIONIST arrives with the tray of drinks and also hands HARVEY an envelope. HARVEY looks surprised and opens it)* I found your tickets. My apologies for the delay. They have been here all the time.

HARVEY: I don't believe it! But you said you couldn't find them? That they hadn't been delivered.

RECEPTIONIST: Ja, this is so. Da war eine Verwechslung. There was a mixup. I'm sorry gentleman but it happened before you arrived. We had to change your double room to two singles.

HARVEY: I think I can guess who that is reserved for.
(HARVEY winks at taps his nose. The RECEPTIONIST ignores it)

BASIL: You didn't tell me you booked us in the same room?

HARVEY: Because at the time, they said that was all that was available. It was that or the street. *(looks at RECEPTIONIST)* So what happened to these? *(waves the tickets)*

RECEPTIONIST: It turns out, they were in the wrong box.

HARVEY: Ah, you mean, in the wrong pigeonhole?
RECEPTIONIST: Ja, this is correct. It was placed under your original room number 24. Please accept my apologies, und diese Runde, this round of drinks are on the hotel. *(THE RECEPTIONIST goes back to reception)*

BASIL: Well, it is your lucky day, a free round of drinks and two sets of tickets! You'd best return the Count's set, in case he thinks you were wasting his time.

HARVEY: There you go again. Do learn. Grab every opportunity as it comes. I'm holding pure gold here. People would do anything to get their hands on these. *(HARVEY looks over at HANS and GÜNTER and beckons them back over. As HANS and GÜNTER sit down HARVEY raises his glass)* Cheers.

GÜNTER & HANS: *(Raise their beer mugs)* Prost!

HARVEY: *(HARVEY smiles, looks over at GÜNTER and waves the envelope)* You know what's in here? *(HARVEY takes the tickets out of the envelope and waves them)*

GÜNTER: Ja. It is incredible!

HARVEY: Yes, especially when I tell you I am going to give them to you. *(HARVEY teases them)* Unless of course you don't want to go to the opening of the games tomorrow? *(GÜNTER confers with HANS in German. Both of them appear to be excited)* You haven't answered my question.

GÜNTER: Question?

HARVEY: Do you want to go or not?

GÜNTER: Ja, very much, of course. We would both very much like to go. It would be... how do you say in English? Like a Traum... Like a dream, a dream come true.

HARVEY: Then we, or should I say I, will have to make your dream come true.

BASIL: Good for you, Harvey! For once, you're doing the decent thing.

HARVEY: Hopefully it'll be the indecent thing, and make all kinds of dreams come true.

BASIL: You can't be serious?

HARVEY: Why not? I told you, grab every opportunity as it comes along. *(as HARVEY goes to hand GÜNTER the envelope. GÜNTER leans forward to take it, HARVEY pulls it back to his chest. (HARVEY looks up toward the landing at the top of the staircase. He then turns and winks at GÜNTER)* I'm sure you've guessed by now... we all have our dreams and fantasies. *(GÜNTER doesn't look pleased)*

BASIL: You're disgusting, that's blackmail.

HARVEY: But I haven't said anything?

BASIL: Then don't. It's despicable... worse, it's just sordid.

HARVEY: Oh, boo hoo. Come off it, they are grown men. And look, it's not exactly stopping them downing the free booze is it? Besides, it's my business how I dispose of these *(GÜNTER and HANS are talking amongst themselves, GÜNTER is not looking at all happy. He takes a bottle of wine and pours some into HANS'S mug)*

BASIL: You really are one arrogant selfsh git! For just once, do something without strings attached. Especially sexual ones.

HARVEY: He's over twenty one, it's his choice. Don't you worry, he'll go for it quite happily. Remember, I'm doing them both a good deed. And it's only fair, good deeds should be rewarded.

BASIL: Then for your sake, let's hope that turns out to be the case.

HARVEY: Oh, come on Basil, don't be such a prude. After all, we are abroad and I promise you, you don't see many like that, on the meat rack in Piccadilly on a rainy night.

BASIL: I would have thought by now, you would have grown out of overnight pickups.

HARVEY: Don't exaggerate, twenty minutes does me.

BASIL: Before it's too late, you should settle down and have a relationship. The way you're going, you'll end up a lonely and no doubt, bitter old queen.

HARVEY: Hate to point it out, but when it comes down to it, you're just envious.

BASIL: You have got to be kidding. Of your wealth? It hasn't brought you much happiness has it?

HARVEY: At times it has... but be honest, it's not my wealth your envious of is it..? It's my freedom.

BASIL: Rubbish! I'm simply saying, you should settle down. After all, you are nearly thirty years old. It'll soon be Bonjour, comment sa va middle age? You flit about from person to person like a bloody butterfly.

HARVEY: *(HARVEY laughs)* At least say it in German. Schmetterling sounds much more masculine. No, if you don't mind. I'll stick to flitting about, enjoying all the beauties nature has to offer.

BASIL: Nothing natural about one-night stands every night.

HARVEY: And I suppose, your monogamous utopia in leafy laned suburbia, *until death you depart,* is so much better? No, I prefer my freedom, rather than depend on somebody else for my happiness.

BASIL: One has to make sacrifices, that's what marriage is about. And who knows, we could soon have children to look forward to.

HARVEY: You straights are so obsessed with breeding... yet, most babies are never planned. After all, a shag is a shag. Maybe you should live here in Germany, they give the mothers medals for it.

BASIL: You really do think of yourself above the norms of society, mocking convention at every turn. When in reality, sexually and emotionally, you are just a spoiled brat who never got past the age of puberty.

HARVEY: *(HARVEY ignores BASIL'S remarks and focuses his attention back to GÜNTER and HANS who are quietly chatting. HANS appears to be getting drunk)* Günter have you considered my offer? As time is running out, I'm sure Berlin is full of young men in uniform, only too willing to chew more than my hand off for these. *(HARVEY waves the tickets at GÜNTER)*

BASIL: Stop this right now, Harvey.

HARVEY: Why? As you just so succinctly put it. It's like a marriage, one has to make sacrifices. Give and take remember? I give him the tickets, he takes them and...

BASIL: And?

HARVEY: *(HARVEY smirks)* And with any luck, by the end of the night, everybody's got what they want... otherwise I may just have to give them back to Von Gantz.

BASIL: You may be drunk, but that's no excuse for being a complete bastard! For goodness sake, do us all a favour and just give them the tickets.

HARVEY: *(HARVEY yawns)* Maybe, but then, maybe I won't.

BASIL: Günter, do you two have anywhere to stay tonight?

GÜNTER: Nein nein, it is too late now... there is nowhere open.

BASIL: Come on Harvey, just him the bloody tickets!

HARVEY: *(HARVEY looks at BASIL)* You're being very boring.

BASIL: And you are being an arse!

HARVEY: You can be such a party pooper.

BASIL: If you don't give him those tickets... I warn you, that'll be the end of our friendship.

HARVEY: Oh, really? If you're going to make such a drama about it, then I might just give them the bloody tickets... Anyway, I'm too tired to argue about it tonight, I'll decide in the morning. *(HARVEY smiles at GÜNTER and waves the tickets, then puts them in his pocket)* But I doubt I'll change my mind.

BASIL: *(BASIL looks at GÜNTER)* In that case, to save this one's reputation, he can stay on the floor in my room.

HARVEY: Alright, if that's the way you want to play it. *(HARVEY turns back to GÜNTER and winks)* Unless, you'd prefer my floor rather than his?

GÜNTER: No.

HARVEY: I thought not. *(HARVEY looks at HANS)* Well old ducks, it seems, as you're not my type, it's your lucky night... you get to stay on my floor... and I mean literally!

BASIL: Okay Günter, come on, if you're staying. *(HARVEY heads towards the stairs with HANS following. HANS looks back and glowers at GÜNTER)*

GÜNTER: *(As GÜNTER goes to head up the stairs. HANS is now looking at him menacingly) GÜNTER appears nervous and stops at the foot of the stairs)* No, wait... this is not right!

BASIL: *(BASIL looks surprised)* What isn't? I promise you, you're perfectly safe with me old mate. I like women, I'm straight. *(GÜNTER doesn't react, he just stands there frozen)* Well, then. If you prefer, you can sleep in those chairs? *(BASIL points to the red leather chairs)* If you pull them together, you can put your feet up. I'll bring you a blanket.

GÜNTER: Danke, I understand this.

BASIL: *(BASIL looks at HARVEY)* Good that's that little the problem solved. I'll bring down a blanket.

GÜNTER: Nein, keine Decke! *(BASIL doesn't seem to understand)*

HARVEY: He says he doesn't want a blanket.

BASIL: *(BASIL is losing patience)* Suit yourself, but don't blame me if you're cold during the night.

GÜNTER: Das ist so. Aber Sie verstehen nicht... *(BASIL looks at HARVEY to interpret)*

HARVEY: He says you don't understand.

BASIL: *(BASIL shrugs his shoulders)* He's right there, I don't. *(BASIL looks back at GÜNTER)* You're safe, staying in my room. But if you don't want to... do us all a favour and just go and sleep in those chairs. *(GÜNTER just stares at him)* I give up! Hans you can stay on my floor then.

HANS: Ja. Danke.

BASIL: (BASIL looks back at GÜNTER) Harvey, you sort him out, I've had enough of his carry on, I'm going to bed.

HARVEY: *(HARVEY looks at GÜNTER)* My friend is right. Go and sleep in the chairs. Gute Nacht. *(HARVEY turns to go)*

GÜNTER: *(to HARVEY)* You understand ja?

HARVEY: Quite frankly old darling, I don't, understand. *(HARVEY gestures to BASIL)* I offered you tickets in exchange for my warm comfortable floor, but you declined my generous offer. He offered you his floor or those chairs... but you still say no.

GÜNTER: Ja, of course. *(HANS is still standing on the staircase, staring menacingly at GÜNTER, whilst taking his eyeline to HARVEY. GÜNTER nervously looks at HANS, then back at HARVEY and raises his voice)* I don't want to stay on his floor, your floor... or those chairs!

HARVEY: Now calm down, lower your voice to a shriek, you'll wake the whole hotel. *(HARVEY walks back down to the foot of the stairs. GÜNTER looks over at HANS)* Then there's only one other choice. *(HARVEY points to the entrance)* and it's out through that door. The street. Good naben.

GÜNTER: *(as HARVEY turns to go back up the stairs. GÜNTER calls after him)* Nein, if the offer is still on, there is one other... Kapiert?
HARVEY: *(HARVEY looks puzzled)* And what would that be?

GÜNTER: I stay in your bed.

HARVEY: *(HARVEY at first looks surprised, he then grins and looks back at BASIL)* Well Basil, it seems I was mistaken. Even in Hitler's Germany, dreams can still come true, albeit for the price of a ticket!

SLOW FADE CURTAIN

ACT II, SCENE I

FOLLOWING AFTERNOON.

HARVEY: *(HARVEY enters from the hotel entrance followed by BASIL)* Bastards! Those bloody evil bastards! *(HARVEY heads to the red leather chairs and slumps down. BASIL sits in the other one)*

BASIL: Just calm down, let's get a drink and gather our thoughts. *(BASIL signals the RECEPTIONIST, indicating he wants a bottle of wine and two glasses)*

HARVEY: Thoughts? I'll tell you my thoughts. I'd like to kill those bastards.

BASIL: For God's sake Harvey, lower your voice. Don't cause any more trouble than you have already. Anyway are you sure it was them?

HARVEY: Of course, it was them, idiot! They were in naval uniform.

BASIL: So were hundreds of others.

HARVEY: Make no mistake, it was them. I ask you? What naval ratings could afford those seats?

BASIL: Yes but you said one of them was wearing glasses, but

77

neither Hans or Günter wore glasses.

HARVEY: That's right one was.

BASIL: There we are then.

HARVEY: What d'you mean, there we are then? Günter did wear glasses.

BASIL: No, he didn't.

HARVEY: He did, for long distances. *(the RECEPTIONIST brings a bottle of wine in an ice bucket and two glasses. He places them on the coffee table)*

BASIL: Then it probably was him.

HARVEY: That's what I've been saying. Who else would it be?

BASIL: Any sign of his mate?

HARVEY: According to the police, he was briefly interrogated, then sent back to their naval base at Bremerhaven.

BASIL: Odd, they would let him go, but not Günter.

HARVEY: Use your brain. Isn't it obvious? Hans informed on him. Probably told them he had slept with me for the tickets.

BASIL: Seems informing, is a German pastime these days… it was definitely Günter you saw?

HARVEY: If you had had the balls to come into the police station, rather than lurk around outside, you would be in no doubt. Even if he was almost unrecognisable.

BASIL: Be fair, there was no point in risking both of us getting locked up. If things had gone wrong for you. I would still have been free to go and get help.

HARVEY: *(sarcastically)* Yes Basil, sounds very plausible.

BASIL: I was only thinking ahead. If they had arrested you, I would have gone to our Embassy for help. *(pauses)* Hold on, if Günter was unrecognisable, then you still can't be absolutely certain it was him?

HARVEY: For God's sake! I said almost. It was in the corridor, as he was being led out to a police van.

BASIL: Well, did he say anything?

HARVEY: How could he? He'd been beaten so badly, his face was just one large bruise, covered in blood. *(HARVEY is extremely upset, he pauses and clears his throat)* His eyelids were so swollen, there was no longer any sign of those piercing blue eyes.

BASIL: Poor kid!

HARVEY: Oddly enough, that crown of golden hair of his, from the front, was still unmistakable… but as he passed, from behind, all you could see was just a tangled mass of matted blood.

BASIL: It just doesn't bear thinking about...

HARVEY: This really vile, fat copper, sitting behind the counter, shouted after him, schmutzig kwiir! Dirty queer. The whole thing was surreal.

BASIL;   Sadistic bastards. Did they say where they were taking him?

HARVEY: Gestapo headquarters for further interrogation. They said his type was usually sent on to some new place, Sachsenhausen. It's a so-called re-education camp. What's really worrying, is that copper laughed, and in German he added, 'And the little poof won't get out of there... nobody does'.

BASIL: So it's a Prison?

HARVEY: No, don't be silly, it's a German version of a Billy Butlin's holiday camp. What do you think it is?

BASIL: You don't have to be sarcastic.

HARVEY: Well then, don't be such an idiot!

BASIL: Your'e right, that was a dumb question.

HARVEY: They said, it's a camp for political prisoners, or anyone else, Hitler's Reich deems undesirable. It was set up this year, and from what I gather, it's far worse than any prison.

BASIL: Poor old Günter, there must be something we can do?

HARVEY: No, but maybe there is something I can do. After all, I am meant to be a journalist. Maybe it's time I proved it.
BASIL: If, as you say, he was almost unrecognisable. Maybe

there is still a small chance it wasn't him?

HARVEY: Be in no doubt old darling. It was him, as obvious, as the name tag, on his bloodstained uniform.

BASIL: Then obviously it was.

HARVEY: Can you believe it?

BASIL: Of course I do.

HARVEY: That they almost ended up sitting in Hitler's lap. They were within handshaking distance... and I'm responsible.

BASIL: Of course you're not.

HARVEY: Of course I am. I gave him von Gantz's tickets! I should have looked at them. It was obvious with his connections, Gantz's seats, would have been better than the ones from my magazine. And they certainly were... bang in the middle of the VIP sector.

BASIL: You can't blame yourself, last night you were pissed, we all were.

HARVEY: Günter wasn't. He had no more than two beers.

BASIL: Come off it. They had several bottles each. Don't forget he was also helping himself to wine and mixing his drinks.

HARVEY: Not his drinks, Hans's drinks. I was watching him. He was trying to get his mate drunk.

BASIL: That doesn't make any sense.

HARVEY: It didn't to me at the time. Don't you see? Günter was trying to get Hans so drunk, he'd pass out. That way, he wouldn't have to sleep with me.

BASIL: Sorry, that's way over my head... Harvey, take my advice before they come looking for us. Let's just pack and get out of here. Remember you too are implicated. After all, you gave him the tickets.

HARVEY: You can go back to London if you want. I'm going to try and do something about getting him free.

BASIL: Now before you do anything rash, just think it through.

HARVEY: Think what through exactly?

BASIL: So far, you've spent your whole life being selfish. I'm telling you, this is not the time to have a change of heart.

HARVEY: But if I were to, I can't think of a better time, can you?

BASIL: Yes, when we are back in London.

HARVEY: Now who's being selfish?

BASIL: Well, it seems they hate homosexuals, as much as Jews. My God, when they find out you had sex with him, we are all for the high jump. They'll think I'm a poof too. We should leave now!

HARVEY: Don't panic old darling... We didn't have sex.
BASIL: What? Well that's a relief. At least they have nothing

to beat out of you.

HARVEY: but we did go to bed together.

BASIL: Oh no, spare me the details.

HARVEY: There aren't any. I lay on my bed in my pyjamas and so as not to crease his uniform, Gunter was in his underwear. Note, I said we were, *on* my bed.

BASIL: That doesn't sound like you.

HARVEY: You're right, it doesn't does it? I have to admit, I was completely bowled over.

BASIL: No surprise there then. After all, you were letching after him all evening.

HARVEY: It's more than that... he's so sweet, so unspoilt.

BASIL: *(sarcastically)* Absolutely fascinating. Now come on let's get going.

HARVEY: He's also, highly intelligent and extremely well read…

BASIL: So should we be, on the train times out of here.

HARVEY: D'you know?

BASIL: *(interrupts)* No, Harvey, luckily I don't know… and frankly I don't want to either.

HARVEY: *(gets quite excited)* You'd be surprised how much

Günter knew about art. Especially, Monet and Piccasso. Not to mention Cubism and Surrealism.

BASIL: Yes well, Surreal is the situation we're in right now. So forgive me, if I don't feign even a modicum of interest in your sex life… as we have to get out of here… now!

HARVEY: *(HARVEY appears not to hear)* He can also be very funny.

BASIL: *(smirks)* Really...? Well there were no signs of any humour last night.

HARVEY: That's because he was being watched.

BASIL: Yes... You never took your eyes off the poor sod.

HARVEY: I mean by Hans. He was also watching him.

BASIL: *(BASIL at first looks puzzled, then scoffs)* Snap out of your daydream. He knew exactly what he was coming to your room for... and it wasn't just for the tickets.

HARVEY: True.

BASIL: There we are then.

HARVEY: He had no choice...

BASIL: Of course he did.

HARVEY: No. Hans made him.
BASIL: But Hans is straight?

HARVEY: Exactly. but Hans suspected Günter wasn't straight, so he used it as leverage. He bullied Günter into getting the tickets. And before you say it, I know this is all my fault.

BASIL: There's no dispute there. As far as blackmail goes, you are as guilty as his mate. You used those tickets as bait, and if you hadn't, we wouldn't be in this mess.

HARVEY: Not quite true, old boy. We are in this mess, because I gave them the wrong tickets.

BASIL: I suppose.

HARVEY: I don't care what you say, I really do like him...

BASIL: This trip is turning out to be a rollercoaster of surprises.

HARVEY: Come on, be honest, Günter's a far cry from what I'm used to... dumb rentboys, who at the very mention of Monet, would think I'm offering them more money, not discussing art. He is just wonderful. In those few hours, I got to know a lot about him... and funny enough, myself as well.

BASIL: (smirks) That must have been quite a revelation.

HARVEY: You can mock, but believe it or not, he managed to get me to take a good hard look at myself, and that's when...

BASIL: You discovered that painting of yourself hidden in the attic... rotting!

HARVEY: That I suffer from low esteem. Anyway, you are being really callous. This is hardly the time to joke.

BASIL: Your'e right, I was just trying to lighten things up.

HARVEY: Well, you ceratinly pick your moments... He also said, I'm an arrogant, selfish waste of space... who dislikes himself.

BASIL: Good for him... Günter said all that?

HARVEY: Well, roughly translated, yes.

BASIL: But that's hardly an epiphany. We've known that for years.

HARVEY: It's not my fault, I suffer from low self-esteem, it's lack of fulfillment... also not enough love and attention as a child.

BASIL: Huh! Oh no, not that old chestnut. You can hardly blame your poor mum for dying, or your dad for not having time to tuck you in. After all, he does have a huge estate to run, he never had the time.

HARVEY: Maybe, but he was right on one thing. I'm not fulfilled. I do nothing productive with my life. Apart from pretending to write recipes for a living. I have no real reason to wake up in the morning. One day is the same as any other... in the end, all for what?

BASIL: Please, don't go on. You'll have me in tears in a minute... and it won't be from crying.

HARVEY: What I'm saying, isn't dependent on your sympathy vote.

BASIL: *(BASIL realises HARVEY is genuinely upset)* I'm sorry, who knows, perhaps it really does take a stranger to show you who you really are.

HARVEY: Yes, and I'm sure with Günter, it could even have developed into something much more... something really special.

BASIL: Well, if that really is the case, do you mind if I delay my shock? That is, until we are safely back in Piccadilly, propping up the Ritz bar? Then perhaps, after downing several Martini's, I maybe just drunk enough to believe there really is a beating heart under your selfish exterior.

HARVEY: Maybe you're right. Maybe it is time for this old butterfly to settle down.

BASIL: Yes, before it's too late.

HARVEY: Sadly, entomologically speaking, I think it already is. Sounds daft, but Günter was the one metophorical pin that could have done it... but now I will never know. But what I do know is, I'm going to do my damndest to get him released.

BASIL: Then maybe you should use this, as a wake up call.

HARVEY: Talking of calls, I'll do that, I'll call von Gantz. Maybe he can sort this mess out. *(HARVEY rummages through his wallet and finds GANTZ'S card)* Excellent. *(HARVEY then goes over to the reception area and speaks to the RECEPTIONIST)* Can you place a call to this number? *(as HARVEY goes to hand the RECEPTIONIST the card, VON GANTZ bursts through the entrance doors, followed by two SS. men)* Von Gantz! The very man. I desperately need to speak to you .

VON GANTZ: *(shouts in German)* Was? Was? You need

what? You ungrateful Dummkopf! You need to speak to me? After what you have done? No, I want to speak to you.

HARVEY: Excellent, then we can sort this whole mess out.

VON GANTZ: *(calms down)* Was? Me, sort this mess out? This mess as you call it, is of your making. You gave your word, as one so-called Gentleman to another. And you broke it.

HARVEY: But I didn't.

VON GANTZ: Correction, you did. You promised to be discrete. But instead, you flouted my generous gift.

HARVEY: But I was discrete, it was a mistake, that's all…

VON GANTZ: *(VON GANTZ interrupts)* That's all? *(shouts)* Even the Fuhrer saw them sitting there! *(calms himself)* Himmler thought they must have been Admiral Donitz's guests. When he discovered they weren't, all hell broke loose. Even I was interrogated as to how they got there. Of course, I didn't know. Then as you English say, the penny dropped. You had given them my tickets. But why? I just don't understand. You almost begged me for them. Then to give them to a couple of whore boys? It doesn't make sense. *(VON GANTZ scoffs)* Ha! For your sake, I hope they were worth it!

HARVEY: I can understand you're annoyed. *(VON GANTZ interrupts)*

VON GANTZ: You can understand? You couldn't possibly understand, you fool! This almost involved the Fuhrer himself!

HARVEY: But it was the hotel's mistake not mine. They lost and then found my original tickets, so, I gave the boys your ones. I foolishly didn't look at them properly, I had no idea how generous you had been. I didn't realise that they were in the VIP section. It was a simple mistake.

VON GANTZ: Simple, simple? This is what you call a simple mistake? *(starts shouting again)* It's catastrophic! It will have all kinds of repercussions.

HARVEY: Please, calm yourself. I'm sorry.

VON GANTZ: Yes, yes, I will calm myself. And now very calmly, I am ordering you to leave Germany, by the very latest tomorrow morning. If at first light, you are still here, then the Gestapo will personally escort you to the airport. For a more comfortable drive, I advise you to leave before they arrive. *(VON GANTZ turns to leave)*

HARVEY: What will happen to Günter ?

VON GANTZ: ˙   Günter? *(VON GANTZ smirks)* His little shipmate told us everything about you and your sailor friend. So he is in the best place... prison.

HARVEY: I saw him at the police station, he was so badly beaten, his own mother wouldn't have recognised him.

VON GANTZ: Don't concern yourself. I advise you do not get involved.

HARVEY: But I already am involved. It's because of me he is there.

VON GANTZ: You should have thought of that, before you

were so generous with my tickets.

HARVEY: I will do as you ask and leave on the first plane. But I need to know, *(raises his voice)* in fact I demand to know what is going to happen to him?

VON GANTZ: *(the SS guards stiffen up)* For your own sake, I advise you not to shout.

HARVEY: *(HARVEY calms himself)* I'm sorry, but having seen what they have done to him, I'm sure you can understand my concerns.

VON GANTZ: As I said, this doesn't concern you.

HARVEY: I'm just asking you, as one civilised Gentleman to another. What will happen to him?

VON GANTZ: What do you think? He is a homosexual! So naturally, he is on his way to a re-education camp

HARVEY: Yes, I've heard Sachsenhausen. They say that few prisoners even survive there...

VON GANTZ: How do you know this?

HARVEY: They told me at the police station.

VON GANTZ: Those idiots, they know nothing! Yes, it is strict and there is discipline. But be reassured, prisoners are well treated. Who knows, if he learns the errors of his ways, he may eventually be released. It will depend on him.

HARVEY: In that case, I will refuse to leave Berlin until he is released. He has done nothing wrong.

VON GANTZ: *(laughs)* He is a degenerate! Well, if you decide to stay. The Gestapo will have to escort you and your friend to the police station. It will be a brief, but I assure you, very unpleasant visit. Then they will stamp your passports, 'Enemies of the Third Reich', before putting you on the first aeroplane headed out of Germany.

HARVEY: Well, then, you give me no choice. You are forgetting, I am an accredited journalist. I will write an article along the lines of how sadistically your Third Reich treats its own citizens.

VON GANTZ: *(roars with laughter)* Accredited? You are indeed. A credit to your magazines cookery section. *(laughs again and heads to the exit)*

HARVEY: *(HARVEY calls after VON GANTZ, who looks back)* Go on, laugh your head off, but that won't stop me. I'll still write something... and it won't be flattering.

VON GANTZ: *(as VON GANTZ heads for the door)* Ja, ja. Go home and in future, stick to the recipes you English are so famous for... Jam Roly Poly Puddings. Oh ja, I and almost forgot, Spotted Dicks of course! *(he laughs and exits)*

BASIL: You were pushing it, Harvey. Anyway at least they are letting us go. Thankfully, he didn't take your threats seriously.

HARVEY: He knows, as a journalist I carry no weight. Seems there is nothing I can do, other than write a letter to *The Times*, or something equally as useless. *(HARVEY pauses)* I promise you this, when we get back, there'll be no more recipes or cooking tips. Just plain old hard hitting journalism, with Germany as my subject matter.

BASIL: Come on, let's go home. Then maybe see what strings your family can pull. At least, he said, Günter has a chance, even if it is slim. In the meantime, try and take your mind off it. Go for a walk, while I start packing.

HARVEY: You're right, I certainly need some fresh air.

BASIL: The sooner we are out of here the better. If we're lucky, we might still be able to catch the night sleeper to Paris.

HARVEY: Good idea! If we leave tonight, that at least gives us a few more hours. *(HARVEY heads out the door as BASIL goes up the stairs)*

(LIGHTS FADE)

ACT II SCENE II

(LIGHTS UP - LOBBY 1 HOUR LATER)

HARVEY: (*HARVEY enters the lobby from the street. He looks dishevelled, his jacket is torn and he has a graze on his face. With him is a shabbily dressed, dark haired woman in her early twenties. HARVEY has his arm around her*) Come on, no reason to be frightened anymore, especially of me. (*EVA tries to pull away*) I promise you, as far as the fairer sex goes, I'm even more harmless than a fly. Now come on.

EVA: (*EVA is very nervous*) I'm sorry, but you do not understand.

HARVEY: Ah, you speak English?

EVA: Yes.

HARVEY: What don't I understand?

EVA: I have to go… it isn't safe.

HARVEY: Nonsense. Come and sit down, you are safer in here, than you were out there. (*HARVEY takes her by the arm and gently leads her past reception and sits her down in one of the red leather chairs. HARVEY sits in the other one)* There we are. Isn't this more comfortable? *(HARVEY goes to to hold her hand, to calm her)*

EVA: *(EVA pulls away from him)* I must not come in here! I am not allowed.

HARVEY: Oh, don't be silly. *(as HARVEY is talking, the RECEPTIONIST walks over)* Now just sit there and try to relax and I'll get you something to drink. *(HARVEY stands up and turns to the RECEPTIONIST)* Ah, just the man! I would like your finest cognac for the lady, best make that a double... and I will have my usual white wine. *(HARVEY looks down at his torn jacket)* On second thoughts, make it two double cognacs, separate glasses.

RECEPTIONIST: Please, Herr Miller, you must take her out of here immediately! She is not allowed in here. Look at the state of her clothes. Please, I have my other guests to consider.

EVA: I will go, I should never have come in here. *(EVA looks at the RECEPTIONIST)* I am sorry.

RECEPTIONIST: That is okay. Good girl, but please, just just go.

HARVEY: *(EVA attempts to stand up but appears to be very shaken. HARVEY gently pushes her back into the chair)* She is going nowhere. You've gotten the wrong end of the stick old man. This is not what you think it is, this girl is respectable. As for the state of her clothes, yours would be the same, if you had just been attacked in the street. She was literally kicked into the gutter! *(HARVEY points to his jacket)* Here, here is proof. Look at my jacket, it's ruined.

RECEPTIONIST: I am sorry, but it is out of the question. *(nervously)* I told you. She is not allowed.

HARVEY: Not allowed? I thought this dump is supposed to be a hotel, not a members only nightclub.

RECEPTIONIST: Please Herr Miller, I tell you, do not make this situation any more difficult.

HARVEY: And I'm telling you. She is staying as my guest.

RECEPTIONIST: You are forcing me to be indelicate. *(the RE-CEPTIONIST beckons HARVEY to come closer)* I am afraid sir, it is not just the way the young lady is dressed.

HARVEY: Then what for goodness sake?

RECEPTIONIST: She is also... *(THE RECEPTIONIST mutters)* Jewish.

HARVEY: Is that just a wild guess? Or are you suddenly an expert on religion?

RECEPTIONIST: Just look at her, I can tell.

HARVEY: All I can tell, is that you are as sick as some of the others around here

RECEPTIONIST: *(RECEPTIONIST speaks softly)* This is not true. I have no opinions either way. I just get on and keep my head down. Anyway, I have seen her before. Out there in the back where we store the rubbish bins. Scrounging, searching them for food. I have had to chase her away several times. She is trouble I tell you.

HARVEY: *(EVA appears to be in a world of her own. She is curled up in the chair, tightly clasping something with both hands)* Well, I can live with trouble... in fact I'm getting used to it. Now before I cause a scene, get us our drinks. And after what you have just told me, some sandwiches would be in order. *(the RECEPTIONIST seems very nervous)* Don't look so worried, no one's going to notice. And I promise, we will be out of here, as soon she's had something to eat. *(the RECEPTIONIST reluctantly nods and heads off to get the drinks and sandwiches. HARVEY kneels down in front of EVA)* Now what have we here that is so precious? *(EVA is clasping a thin gold chain)* I can't believe anyone would attack you for this little chain. *(HARVEY takes out a handkerchief and gently rubs dirt off EVA'S face)* In England Boy Scouts usually help old ladies across the road. They don't beat up young women, even if they are wearing a Star of David. Best tuck it away, before the innkeeper see's it.

EVA: *(EVA tucks the chain down the back of the chair)* They were not Boy Scouts or Hitler Youth, they were Braunhemden.

HARVEY: Whatever the colour of their shirts were. Brown, pink or lilac. To me, they looked like overgrown Boy Scouts. I must admit, I rather enjoyed giving them a taste of their own medicine. First good scrap I've had since picking up the wrong guardsmen.

EVA: Sorry my English?

HARVEY: Don't trouble your head about it. Just an occupational hazard of mine. It's good to keep in practice. First time it's come in useful for ages. *(HARVEY pushes back EVA'S hair and touches a bruise on her forehead)* Those bully boys really were trying to hurt you.

EVA: Ouch!!

HARVEY: Am so sorry. *(the RECEPTIONIST arrives back with the drinks and sandwiches on a tray. He doesn't look pleased. He dumps them on the table and leaves. EVA doesn't wait, she is obviously starving. She grabs a couple of sandwiches and pushes them into her mouth)* Hey, now slow down. You don't have to rush, they are all for you. No one is going to take them away. Now sip some of this. *(HARVEY hands her a glass of cognac, she takes a sip)* Try and drink it. *(EVA sips some more cognac)* It'll do you good. There, see, it's already brought colour to your cheeks. *(EVA smiles)* I don't even know your name. I'm Harvey. As you may have guessed, I am from England.

EVA: I am Eva, *(EVA whispers)* Eva Goodmann. *(EVA reaches out and nervously touches his cheek)* Your eye is bruised. (EVA seems embarrassed and removes her hand) I must go now, I have caused you enough trouble.

HARVEY: *(HARVEY touches his eye)* Aah, this is what's known in England, as a shiner. Many of my friends would think it's not before time, I got one.

EVA: My father says England, it is very beautiful. As a young man, he taught German there. That is how I learn my English, from him.

HARVEY: Good old Papa! Yes, England is beautiful. I've certainly grown to appreciate it even more so on this trip

EVA: Sorry?

HARVEY: It's a long story.

EVA: I know, I cannot ever repay your kindness, but before I leave, I would like to say thank you. *(EVA gets up to leave. HARVEY gently pushes her back in the chair)* Where do you think you're going?

EVA:　　　　I have to go. I cannot stay here, it is too dangerous.

HARVEY:　　Stop saying that. From what I've seen *(HARVEY touches his eye)* the street is even worse. Don't you have a friend who could put you up?

EVA:　　　　No.

HARVEY:　　There must be someone?

EVA:　　　　No.

HARVEY:　　Your Family?

EVA:　　　　No, they went away.

HARVEY:　　They just up and left? Surely, you have their address?

EVA:　　　　I don't know where they are.

HARVEY:　　Have you been to the police?

EVA:　　　　Of course not. They would arrest me.

HARVEY:　　Why? What have you done?

EVA:　　　　Nothing.

HARVEY:　　They can't just disappear.

EVA:　　　　In Germany they can.

HARVEY: When did you last see them?

EVA: About three months ago. I was on my way home, when I saw soldiers outside our house. They were forcing my parents and my ten year old brother onto a lorry at gunpoint. When my my father pleaded with them to stop, a soldier beat him with his rifle. I was so scared, I hid in a doorway.

HARVEY: My God, what's happening to this country?

EVA: My little brother tried to help, by hitting an SS officer. The officer just laughed and handed him a sweet before beating him unconscious and tossing his lifeless body onto the lorry, like a carcass of meat. Then just as my parents scrambled on to help him, the truck drove off. I ran after it, shouting for them to take me as well. But no one heard. Then a neighbour scurried by and whispered that the SS officer had said something about taking them to a re-education camp.

HARVEY: Yes, that's seems to be what they are calling them these days.

EVA: You have heard of them?

HARVEY: Unfortunately. So where have you been hiding?

EVA: Anywhere I can. (*EVA eats another snadwich as she looks down at her filthy clothes*) As you can see.

HARVEY: Your English is excellent.

EVA: I also speak Russian, some French as well as Hebrew and Yiddish. Languages runs in our family. (*EVA takes more sand-*

wiches) Excuse my manners, but this is the first decent food I've had in weeks. I have been living off apples and berries from people's gardens. Also the occasional scraps from dustbins

HARVEY: Sadly, it's only a sandwich, I will try to do better than that. *(Eva smiles)* Now, as far as this camp goes, if it's the same one, then it's outside of Berlin somewhere. But it's rather hush hush, they won't allow anyone near it. They say it is for the re-education of dissidents. Anyone the Nazis consider to be anti-social, Communists, sexual deviants, whatever.

EVA: And of course Jews. If that is where they are, the rumours about that place are very bad.

HARVEY: It's just impossible to comprehend, being sent to a place like that, just for being Jewish?

EVA: No, not just for being Jewish. My parents are also intellectuals.

HARVEY: That makes even less sense. Surely that is in their favour?

EVA: At the beginning, yes it was.

HARVEY: What did they do?

EVA: My mother was a professor of mathematics, my father a professor in languages and physics. Three years ago they were sacked from their posts. Jews are not allowed to teach in universities anymore. Overnight they lost their livelihoods.

HARVEY: Extraordinary... it's all madness.

EVA: Luckily, a good friend of my father's, a non-Jewish scientist, got them both a job in his laboratory. They worked hard and the hours were long, but they loved it. It was challenging work and worthwhile.

HARVEY: Then, it just doesn't make sense they have been imprisoned. Obviously, there has been a mistake?

EVA: No, there has been no mistake.

HARVEY: Maybe the SS took the wrong family? Got the wrong name, or a wrong address even?

EVA: No, it was the right name and the correct address.

HARVEY: It could of course, be just a bureaucratic slip-up.

EVA: No, it isn't. A couple of months ago, my father was called to his friend's office. He said he wanted my father to work with him on something new the Nazis were developing. It was all top secret. At first, he was very excited, it was another challenge. But then, when my father heard more details about the project, he couldn't continue. He said he wouldn't work on something so unbelievably destructive.

HARVEY: What on earth was it?

EVA: I have no idea. Something, that if built, could kill hundreds, maybe even thousands of people. So naturally, he refused, and my parents were sacked yet again. A few days later, that was when the SS arrived at our house. You know the rest. *(EVA clasps her glass of cognac)* I am so tired of hiding, living in fear, knowing all too well, eventually they will catch me... I just want to go home.

HARVEY: Not advisable: They are bound to be watching your house.

EVA: No, not my family home... my spiritual home.

HARVEY: Where on earth does that reside, if indeed such a place exists?

EVA: It doesn't yet... but it will.

HARVEY: I suppose mine already does. It's the Ritz bar in London. And when I get home, that's the first place I am heading. Where's your spiritual home going to be?

EVA: Palestine.

HARVEY: Palestine? Well that shouldn't be a problem. After all, it is British. Well, under some U.N. mandate or other.

EVA: It has always been my parents dream to go there and establish a Jewish homeland. Now it is my dream.

HARVEY: As it happens, I have one or two contacts at the foriegn office, maybe they could do something. No promises, but we can at least give it a go.

BASIL: *(BASIL comes down the stairs)* Okay, that's done, we're all packed and ready. *(at first BASIL doesn't notice EVA curled up in the chair)* How was your walk? Feeling any better?

HARVEY: Much better. You could say, I feel like a new man.

BASIL: Oh please... this is no time for jokes.

HARVEY: I'm not joking.

BASIL: Good. Well come on then, let's check out the train times and book that sleeper. *(BASIL notices EVA)* Oh, hello? And who are you? *(EVA doesn't respond. BASIL turns to HARVEY and whispers)* Who is she old man? If you ask me, it looks like she could do with a good bath. Have you seen the state of her. She's filthy!

HARVEY: Yes Basil, as a matter of fact I have. Now, let me ask you a question? Were you serious when you said, I should settle down and get married?

BASIL: You have to admit, it has to be better than the way you've been living your life so far.

HARVEY: Let's not have another debate on my sex life. A simple yes or no will suffice.

BASIL: Well then, it's a simple yes.

HARVEY: Another question. Would you say you are my best friend?

BASIL: I'd say, I'm your only friend. Let's face it, there is no one else, eager to take that dubious honour away from me.

HARVEY: Then I have an even more stupid question. Would you be my best man?

BASIL: You mean, as in, if you were ever married? If that day ever comes... yes, with pleasure. *(BASIL scoffs)*. But, got bad news for you, old boy, you can't marry a man. I suggested monogamy not marriage. Now, come on, let's start moving our baggage.

HARVEY: I'm serious. Would you be my best man? If it were a woman?

BASIL: Well of course. If that unlikely event ever occurred. *(chuckles)* But I won't be investing money in a new morning suit anytime soon.

HARVEY: That's okay. I was thinking of a more casual affair. No church wedding for me.

BASIL: What a relief for religion that will be.

HARVEY: Right! So that's a yes then. If I find the right woman of course.

BASIL: It certainly would be! If only to see the expression on our friends and especially your family's faces. Okay, enough of all this nonsense. Come on, let's get the bags and sort out the train times.

HARVEY: Not so fast, you haven't said hello to Eva. *(BASIL looks surprised)*

BASIL: I just did.

HARVEY: But I haven't introduced you properly.... Basil Hopkins this is Eva Goodmann. Eva Goodmann, this is Basil Hopkins. *(EVA and BASIL nervously smile at each other)* Don't be shy.
BASIL: *(BASIL seems embarrassed)* Oh, hello. *(BASIL goes to put out his hand, but notices how dirty Eva's hands are, so he puts his*

hands behind his back instead) Come on, Harvey, it's important we sort this out now. We have to book those tickets before it's too late.

HARVEY: I couldn't agree more.

EVA: *(EVA hasn't been listening to what HARVEY had been saying. Instead, just strokes the wing of the red leather chair)* These chairs are very beautiful, so soft and comfortable, I could live in them.

HARVEY: *(HARVEY kneels down and looks at her)* Eva, look at me. Eva? *(EVA turns and looks at HARVEY)* If that's what you really want. But I have a much better idea… I grant you a little crazy, but it just might work.

EVA: There is only one thing that can work. I have to turn myself into the police. I am too tired to go on like this.

HARVEY: Don't be such a pessimist. Look on the bright side.

EVA: *(EVA looks puzzled)* What bright side? There is no bright side.

HARVEY: There certainly is....

EVA: No, sadly there is not.

HARVEY: Marry me!

BASIL: No!
HARVEY: Shut up, Basil, I wasn't asking you. Eva, did you hear what I just said? I'm serious. Marry me.

EVA: You are making fun of me. I go now. *(EVA gets up and heads toward the exit. HARVEY chases after her)*

HARVEY: *(HARVEY grabs hold of her)* Just Stop! On the contrary, I'm not making fun of you... I promise. I am deadly serious. Just think about it for a moment. This really could work. I know on the face of it, it sounds mad. But you have to admit, it's not half as mad, as you turning yourself into the police, which in turn, will mean the Gestapo.

EVA: *(EVA is surprised)* But I don't even know you. How could this possibly work? We have only just met. I know nothing about you. All I know is, you boast you have friends in high places, and you don't even like women?

HARVEY: It's true, I do have connections. And as for women go, I like them well enough, but just not in that way. Besides all that doesn't matter a fig! Don't you see? It's your ticket out of here!

EVA: I do not see. I am Jew. Are you a Jew?

HARVEY: No, not at all. I'm good old Church of England.

EVA: Then it is illegal in Germany. A Jew cannot marry an Aryan. We would both be in trouble.

HARVEY: For a German, maybe. But I am a good old Anglo-Saxon English Celt. So it doesn't apply.

EVA: *(EVA looks confused)* Why would you marry me? You are a crazy man.

HARVEY: There we are, now we're in agreement. *(HARVEY*

106

gently steers EVA back to the chair and sits her back down) Crazy I maybe, and I know this idea sounds even crazier, but as I said, it just might work!

EVA: No, I should go. *(she stands up again)*

HARVEY: Do stop saying that!

BASIL: Marriage? Harvey, you are joking?

HARVEY: No, I'm not. Basil trust me. It's a long story. All you need to know is she is in grave danger. I'll explain it all later. But for now, just bear with me. I think I've found the answer. *(HARVEY turns back to EVA)* Eva, just listen to me carefully. You agree, you are not safe in Germany?

EVA: Of course.

HARVEY: So let me at least try and get you out. Surely, it's worth a try? We have nothing to lose.

EVA: You do.

HARVEY: As you said, I boasted I have connections.

EVA: But I do not love you.

HARVEY: Excellent! I don't love you either. In fact, I've never loved anyone. Come to think of it, not even myself. And I'm certainly not about to change. *(chuckles)* Well maybe I'll fall in love with myself at some point. This is not about love, it's about getting you to safety. A British passport. And who knows, eventually to your Utopia.

EVA: My Utopia?

HARVEY: Palestine. (EVA looks surprised) You know... Judea, or Israel, or whatever you decide to call it.

EVA: You would do this? But why?

HARVEY: Good question. But I'm not sure of the answer to that. I don't know, blame him. *(HARVEY gestures to BASIL)* Maybe it is time, I did something without strings attached. Do a good deed and hang the consequences and all that.

BASIL: Well for all our sakes, let's hope this good deed, really does go unpunished. I dread to think what the consequences could be if we don't get out of here... you really have lost your marbles.

HARVEY: Eva, all I'm asking from you, is a simple yes or no? Will you consent to being my wife? *(EVA looks at HARVEY)* Come on, we are running out of time.

EVA: *(EVA pauses for a moment and then laughs)* You crazy, crazy Englishman man. Okay. Yes!

HARVEY: Eva Miller...The Honourable Mrs Harvey Cecil-Miller. It sounds good, yes?

EVA: It is unbelievable.

BASIL: It certainly is.
HARVEY: Well, Eva, if you don't like Miller, you can always change it when you get to Palestine. You can get a divorce and find a real husband. *(HARVEY looks at BASIL, who still appears shocked)*

Basil, while I get things sorted here, do me a favour. Nip out and buy her some fresh clothes. *(HARVEY takes out some cash from his wallet)*

BASIL: But I don't know how to buy womens clothes?

HARVEY: Very easy, choose something tasteful, but also good for travelling and with this, you pay for them. *(HARVEY hands BASIL some cash)*

BASIL: But we don't know her size?

HARVEY: What do you think? Extra large? Look at her. *(BASIL looks at EVA)* Small of course! *(BASIL heads out of the hotel)* Eva, come with me. *(HARVEY escorts EVA to the reception area. Where the RECEPTIONIST looks worried)* Don't worry, Herr Smiler, your worries are nearly over. As promised, we are leaving soon. *(HARVEY puts his arm around EVA)* Besides, congratulate me. I'm getting married.

RECEPTIONIST: Ja, ja, now please go now...

HARVEY: I am serious. This young lady has consented to be my wife. *(the RECEPTIONIST looks surprised)* She is going to become British no less! And, as they say, it's a first class ticket to the world.

BASIL: Oh, Harvey...

HARVEY: Eva, this is the key to my room. When Basil brings your new clothes, you can use it to change. The bathroom is on the same floor, so go clean yourself up, while I sort this out *(EVA takes they key and goes upstairs)*

RECEPTIONIST: So it is true?

HARVEY: Yes, afraid so old darling.

RECEPTIONIST: That you British really are mad.

HARVEY: That's as may be, but more importantly, I need your help, old darling.

RECEPTIONIST: Whatever it is, I don't want to hear.

HARVEY: It's only a small favour, and you will be amply rewarded for your trouble. Very amply rewarded. *(HARVEY brings out his wallet and starts peeling off Reichsmarks and British Pounds)* I promise, we will be gone before you know it.

RECEPTIONIST: *(the RECEPTIONIST on seeing the money begin to pile up on his desk smiles and nods in agreement)* Ja, I'm sure we can come to, as you say, a very amicable arrangement.

HARVEY: Good. Now, quick as you can, get on the phone and find us a compassionate priest, with an equally healthy fascination with Reichsmarks and British Pounds.

SLOW FADE CURTAIN

ACT II SCENE III

YEAR 1948. DAYTIME. SAME HOTEL LOBBY, LOOKING VERY SHABBY AND DUSTY WITH SOME MINOR SIGNS OF BOMB DAMAGE.

(EVA enters from the hotel entrance. She is looking a few years older and is elegantly dressed. There is no sign of anyone. She looks around. Apart from the dust and slight damage, everything looks the same. EVA makes a beeline for the red leather chairs and sits down and relaxes, as if taking in the atmosphere. She then slides her hand under the back of one of the cushions. While she is rummaging, the RECEPTIONIST appears from behind the reception desk. He too has aged a little)

RECEPTIONIST: Guten Tag, Fraulein. Can I help you?

EVA: Cognac, bitte.

RECEPTIONIST: Ja, sofort!

EVA: You speak English yes?

RECEPTIONIST: Ja.

EVA: On second thoughts, make it a double cognac. In fact, make it two double cognacs, in two separate glasses. *(the RE-CEPTIONIST nods and walks back to the reception area to get them. In the meantime EVA continues to search under the cushion for some-*

thing. As the RECEPTIONIST returns with a tray. EVA stops immediately. He places the drinks on the coffee table in front of the chairs)

RECEPTIONIST: You have been here before, yes?

EVA: Yes, yes I have. It was before the war.

RECEPTIONIST: Yes of course! *(looks around)* Before my lovely hotel was reduced to this? I thought I recognised you. Now let me see. Before the war you say?

EVA: Yes, you tried to throw me out of here, remember?

RECEPTIONIST: Me? No! I have never thrown any of my guests out of here. This must be someone else you are thinking of. *(the RECEPTIONIST looks into a mirror and straightens his tie)*

EVA: Well, if that wasn't you. It must have been that doppelganger, you are staring at in that mirror. Maybe time is playing tricks on your memory.

RECEPTIONIST: Of course, it isn't. I have a good memory for faces, and I can promise you, we have never met. I would have recognised you instantly!

EVA: Well, when I say I stayed here, I wasn't a guest as such. I just sat here in this chair, sipping cognac and eating sandwiches. It was for just a few hours. Maybe that is why you don't remember.

RECEPTIONIST: Ah, yes of course, that would be it.

EVA: You got very angry and told me I wasn't allowed to sit here. Surely you remember now? *(EVA begins rummaging behind the cushion again)*

RECEPTIONIST: Why would I be angry because you sat there? Guests are guests, they sit where they like. It makes no sense. Just because you sat there, rather than over there? *(the RECEPTIONIST points toward the chairs by the semi boarded up window)*

EVA: You were frightened.

RECEPTIONIST: Frightened... frightened of you? It makes no sense.

EVA: *(EVA finally finds what she was searching for. It is her gold chain with the Star of David. EVA holds it up to show the RECEPTIONIST)* This is why you were frightened of me. And this is why, on this very day, you tried to throw me out. August 1st 1936... exactly twelve years ago. The first day of the Olympics... Remember?

RECEPTIONIST: Ah ja... now I remember. You were a Jew. I had no choice. It was the law. Mein Gott! Look how you have changed.

EVA: My clothes maybe. But not me, I haven't... I'm still a Jew. *(EVA looks at her gold chain)* To think this is still here after so long.

RECEPTIONIST: It has been there all this time? But how?

EVA: I hid it in the cushion.

RECEPTIONIST: You came back, just for that?

EVA: Not just for this. But also for one last look around at where, thanks to that wonderful Englishman, my dreams and present nightmares all began... You must remember him?

RECEPTIONIST: Yes, of course. I could never forget him. He was so crazy. How could anyone forget him... or the wedding. (he pauses) Yes, and don't you forget, it was me that helped you, remember? It was me who arranged for the priest and served you my best champagne. I put myself in grave danger for you.

EVA: Yes, of course I remember, and no, it wasn't for me. You and that drunken priest did it for the money. You even took Harvey's gold signet ring.

RECEPTIONIST: He insisted. It was, how do you say in English? It was my tip. For my services.

EVA: It was because you took all his cash. He had nothing else to pay you with.

RECEPTIONIST: I was taking a big risk. I could have gotten into terrible trouble. I am sorry for how I treated you, but it's all so long ago now. You must realise, I had no choice. The Nazis would have made trouble for me. They had spies everywhere.

EVA: (EVA clasps her glass with both hands and settles back in the chair) Yes, it does all seem a long time ago. The last twelve years have passed so quickly, and so many things have happened. I'm not blaming you for wanting me out of here. It's how things were. At least you gave me time to have a bath and change my clothes... more importantly... to feel human again. To be fair, Herr Smiler, as you say, you did help save my life

RECEPTIONIST: Ha! That is what he used to call me. But I don't know why. My name is Wolfgang.

EVA: Probably because you are always smiling.

RECEPTIONIST: *(looks serious)* Yes that must be it. So will you and your husband be staying? At the moment I only have four usable rooms. But they are nice rooms. The others still need painting and some repairs from the bombing. I take it your husband will be arriving soon?

EVA: No, that glass is not for him. It is for you. To drink a toast.

RECEPTIONIST: Drink a toast? To what?

EVA: To our absent friend... the Honourable Harvey Cecil - Miller.

RECEPTIONIST: But I wasn't really his friend?

EVA: Perhaps not, but he paid you enough to be. And after all, you were a witness at our wedding.

RECEPTIONIST: So he is not coming? I take it he is still in England?

EVA: Yes, I'm afraid he is. *(EVA raises her glass)* Come on, Wolfgang, raise your glass. *(THE RECEPTIONIST picks up the other glass of cognac and raises it)* To the Honourable Harvey Cecil-Miller. The most wonderful man, that I was privileged to marry.

RECEPTIONIST: *(he shrugs)* To Herr Harvey. Prost!

EVA: That day, Harvey dragged me off that street. The first thing he did was to make me drink this, to warm me up. After just a few sips my head began to spin. But it didn't matter. *(EVA snuggles up in the chair)* After months of sleeping on the pavement, or huddled up in doorways, just to be able to sit somewhere and get warm, in something so comfortable as these chairs, it was unimaginable. For so long now, I wanted to come back, just to see where, exactly twelve years ago today, I got married. *(EVA raises her glass)* So, to my wedding aniversary!

RECEPTIONIST: *(Seems surprised and rasises his glass)* Today is you wedding anneversary? Prost!

EVA: *(EVA changes the subject)* Are they very old?

RECEPTIONIST: Sorry?

EVA: The chairs.

RECEPTIONIST: Yes, they are very old *(the RECEPTIONIST sits in the other chair and rubs the arm)*

EVA: I cannot believe after all this time, they are still here.

RECEPTIONIST: They nearly were not. My hotel just missed a direct hit on the last month of the war. It ruined the foundation of the building. Each year, it gets worse. Look, look at the dust everywhere. I do my best to clean, but it's useless. It is plasterwork slowly cracking and dropping everywhere. That is why the place is empty. The auctioneers are coming next week, to see what can be salvaged and sold off. Then I don't know where I will go.

EVA: I really am sorry to hear that. *(the RECEP-TIONIST nods in appreciation)* Just imagine, if these chairs could speak, the stories they could tell.

RECEPTIONIST: Yes there would be many. But I am sure, not all would be like yours and have such a happy ending.

EVA: I'm sorry, was that the impression I gave?

RECEPTIONIST: Well, you did say you achieved your dream. Not many can say that.

EVA: True, but at a higher cost than I could ever have imagined.

RECEPTIONIST: Well, at least we made it through the war... Prost!

EVA: Yes, we did that. (they clink glasses)

RECEPTIONIST: Let's be grateful... millions didn't.

EVA: I know that all too well. My family didn't, they died in Bergen-Belsen, just weeks before the British arrived... L'Chaim! *(as they sip the cognac, EVA looks around)* It is so sad, you are closing my favorite hotel.

RECEPTIONIST: I have to, before it falls down and closes itself.

EVA: So you are putting everything in auction?

RECEPTIONIST: Yes, whatever is not damaged. I have managed to sell some things already.

EVA: I would happily give you a very good price for these chairs.

RECEPTIONIST: (smiles) Nothing would give me greater pleasure, but I have just sold them to an English officer. He is billeted just across the square. His wife is taking them back to England. The chairs are English.

EVA: Well then, I can hardly disapprove. After all, they are going home.

RECEPTIONIST: If there is anything else you would like to buy?

EVA: Just another cognac.

RECEPTIONIST: (the RECEPTIONIST takes the bottle from the reception desk and walks back and pours them both more cognac) Well then, let's have another toast. I know, to survival!

EVA: Yes and to my husband. Without whom I would never have reached England and survived.

RECEPTIONIST: Yes, prost! You live there now, yes? It is nice?

EVA: Yes it is, it is very beautiful. But no, I don't.

RECEPTIONIST: Why? If it is so beautiful.

EVA: You are forgetting, our marriage was just a charade to get me out of here. As soon as I received my naturalisation documents, I applied for a British Passport. When it came through, Harvey then told me to go for an annulment.

RECEPTIONIST: Vas ist diese?

EVA: It's like a divorce, but instead, it cancels the marriage completely... as if it never happened.

RECEPTIONIST: But why? On what grounds?

EVA: On the grounds the marriage was never consummated.

RECEPTIONIST: Ja, a typical Englishman. I remember those sailors. Degenerates. You were right to divorce him.

EVA: That wasn't the reason. He told me his sexual preferences the moment we met. He never wanted to make love to me. He just wanted to save my life... and he succeeded.

RECEPTIONIST: Sounds like you feel guilty divorcing him. But there was no future in it.

EVA: We never divorced. Neither of us ever got around to signing the annulment papers. *(the RECEPTIONIST pours another drink)* By the time they came through, I was in Palestine.

RECEPTIONIST: How could you be so busy, as not to sign your own divorce papers?

EVA: I suppose, deep down I didn't want to. I had become rather fond of him. After all, I owed him my life... I didn't realise it at the time, but I had grown to love him.

RECEPTIONIST   But that is crazy, he was....

EVA: Homosexual? Yes. He was also the perfect husband. Kind, affectionate, and moreover, fun to be with... *(EVA looks at the chairs)* in many ways, we were a bit like these... a perfect match.

RECEPTIONIST   *(scoffs)* But a woman needs a real man. You know what I mean, a man who can satisfy her.

EVA: Well, in every other way he did, and he was certainly a man... more of a man than most. And if sex would have become important, I was never to find out, as by then I had joined the Haganah.

RECEPTIONIST: Haganah?

EVA: It is a para-military organization, set up to defend Jewish settlements, from attacks from Palestinian Arabs. Then soon after, we had to fight the British.

RECEPTIONIST: The British? But they fought the Nazis. They helped save the Jews. It doesn't make sense.

EVA: I suppose that was the 'geshpet' of the situation.

RECEPTIONIST: Geshpet?

EVA: The irony. They began to restrict Jewish immigration and wanted to grant Palestine independence, with an Arab majority. We had no choice but to fight. So I joined the Irgun,

RECEPTIONIST: Haganah? Irgun? All these names?

EVA: We were freedom fighters, but to the British, we were a so-called terrorist group. We became experts at sabotage. Blowing up bridges, railway lines, even the ships the British were using for Jewish deportations. And of course, the King David Hotel. You may have read about that. It got a lot of publicity.

RECEPTIONIST   Everybody heard about it. they say a lot of innocent people were killed, including Jews.

EVA: Yes, that was a big mistake. But then, in our struggle for a homeland, I was guilty of making more than just one mistake.

RECEPTIONIST: These things can happen in war. From what I have read, you have now achieved your Jewish homeland.

EVA: Yes, this year, three months ago. On May 14th, at the stroke of midnight, the British mandate was over. Eleven minutes later, President Truman recognised us as the State of Israel.

RECEPTIONIST: Congratulations, you were obviously very committed.

EVA: We had to be, there was so much to organise, so many things to learn. How to use mortars, machine guns, how to handle explosives, even how to repair engines. Not to mention, how to get information out of informers, taking hostages and planning raids. There wasn't a moment of the day wasted.

RECEPTIONIST: Didn't your husband object to all this? After all, he is British.

EVA: He had no idea I had joined the Irgun. He thought I was just growing vegetables and teaching English on a kibbutz. He was also busy. By then, he had become a successful journalist, having published the story of his stay in Berlin. It proved to be a huge success. Soon after, he became a war correspondent for *The Times* newspaper no less.

RECEPTIONIST: I am sure, he must enjoy doing that. Better than cooking recipes. It is more masculine.

EVA: He loved being a war correspondent, on D-Day he was in the thick of it. It seems he had at last found his forte. After the war, he would send me postcards from all over the place, Indonisia, Greece, Korea, Malaya. Wherever there were wars, or battles going on. Even New York... But that was to cover a U.N. meeting about starving refugees in Europe.

RECEPTIONIST: America? Ja, I wish I had gone before the war… *(sighs)* too late now.

EVA: Soon after his trip to New York, I received a letter from England. He said he was coming to report on, what the British called, the unrest in Palestine. Said it was a very hush-hush. *(EVA smiles)* Those English with their funny expressions.

RECEPTIONIST: Yes I know. Stupid. *(the RECEPTIONIST attempts to impersonate an English accent)* What-ho old boy! Jolly good show! Cheerio, old duck. What is all this matey, shows and ducks? It makes no sense.

EVA: *(EVA smiles again)* No it doesn't, does it…. But then, *(EVA's thoughts seem to be somewhere else)* many things we do, don't make sense. Where was I?

RECEPTIONIST: Palestine. You were saying your husband was going to join you in Palestine.

EVA: He was, but with, all that was happening there, along with all the bureaucracy, I never did get to hear when he was due to arrive.

RECEPTIONIST: So you never saw him.

EVA: Yes, I did... quite by chance.

RECEPTIONIST: You must have had a lot to talk about.

EVA: We certainly did, but we never spoke.

RECEPTIONIST: Ah, so he did find out you had been fighting against the British? It is understandable. I would do the same.

EVA: No, he never knew.

RECEPTIONIST: Then, why didn't he speak to you?

EVA: He was too far away.

RECEPTIONIST: But you said you saw him?

EVA: Yes, at a distance, but I didn't recognise him, If I had, I would have waved, or shouted something to get his attention.   .

RECEPTIONIST: When did you next see him?
EVA   I was never to see him again... alive that is. A few weeks later, I received a letter, along with a small parcel from the War Office in London, informing me he was dead. In the parcel was a small box containing his personal effects. Some of my letters and this photograph of him in uniform. *(EVA takes a photograph from her bag and hands it to the RECEPTIONIST)* By then, as you can see,

Harvey had the rank of lieutenant. He looks so smart in his British khaki and officer's cap that he's barely recognisable. Don't you think? *(the RECEPTIONIST looks at the photograph and nods in agreement)* It took a while for it to sink in, that it really was Harvey. I had only ever seen him dressed in his English tailored suits.

RECEPTIONIST: Yes, well he was a stylish man.

EVA: True, but it's strange, how men in uniform all seem to look the same.

RECEPTIONIST: *(the RECEPTIONIST hands EVA back the photograph)* Yes, yes, I suppose they do. Did they say how he died?

EVA: The letter read, that he had been on patrol in an armoured car when it was attacked by, what they referred to as, a band of Jewish terrorists. One of them, had thrown a hand-grenade. although it was a near miss, the explosion, caused the car to go out of control and hit a tree, before catching on fire. When I read that letter, I did something I hadn't done in years. I cried.

RECEPTIONIST: I'm so sorry.

EVA: For weeks, I just sat around sobbing, trying to figure out some way of bringing his killer to justice… but all that grieving-didn't help. I knew the only real way was… *(EVA goes into Yiddish)* Iz an aoyg far an ayog. *(The RECEPTIONIST is puzzled)* It's Yiddish. An eye for an eye… in other words, kill the person responsible.

RECEPTIONIST: I see, and did you?

EVA: Nearly… I thought of all kinds of ways to go about it. Yet, when it came to the crunch… I never had the guts to go through with it. So I just live with the guilt... and it doesn't get any easier.

RECEPTIONIST: But why?

EVA: Because feeling guilty, doesn't come close enough to do him justice.

RECEPTIONIST: And killing his assassin, in the end, what would that have achieved?

EVA: Justice.

RECEPTIONIST: For Herr Miller, maybe… and for you?

EVA: Peace...

RECEPTIONIST: Hah! You are so hard on yourself, I don't understand?

EVA: You might, when I tell you the name of the person who threw that hand grenade... *(in Yiddish)* Rosh Kvutza Goodmann. *(the RECEPTIONIST is still baffled)* .... Corporal *Eva* Goodmann

RECEPTIONIST: Are you saying...?

EVA: Yes, I'm saying exactly that. It was me... I was the one who killed him.

LIGHTS DIM. CURTAIN.

Allan Warren

The Matching Pair - Part 1: No Good Deed

* 9 7 8 0 9 5 5 5 6 3 1 8 8 *